Rhododendrons, Camellias & Magnolias 2022

GW00566108

RHS
Rhododendron, Camellia
& Magnolia Group

Contents

Rhododendron luteiflorum '**Glencoy**' (p32)

Magnolia '**Sunset Swirl**' (p48)

Camellia '**Hongtian Xiangyun**'
('**Red Sky with Fragrant Cloud**') (p67)

Camellia **'Firebird'** (p92)

Rhododendron cumberlandense (p106)

Magnolia **'Esther'** (p128)

Chairman's foreword

Graham Mills

I concluded my foreword in the 2021 yearbook by expressing belief that before I wrote the next one 'the pandemic should be under control and normal activities will have resumed'. How wrong one can be! Last year played out as a repeat of the previous with very few face-to-face activities.

However, one of the positives is that we have fully embraced using the internet to advance and enhance our activities. Virtual talks have become a regular feature, thanks to the efforts of **Wendelin Morrison**, and we once again held a most successful Centenary Cup Competition via the Group website. The number of individuals connecting with us through our Social Media presence has expanded enormously as a result of the efforts of **Mark Bobin**. Due to these activities and with our new website, I feel that we are better serving and engaging with all our members, irrespective of their country or the season. Despite this, these internet-based facilities should not lead to us overlooking the value of our well-regarded yearbook and bulletins in spreading the word about our three genera.

This year may well prove my previous optimistic view of the pandemic right. We have already had our first show in the UK at Rosemoor and visits organised by the various branches are taking place. It's good to see people getting together again. Preparations for the AGM and the Centenary Cup Competition are well in hand. After two years when of necessity it has been a virtual event, the AGM will take place at Ramster Garden in Chiddingford, Surrey, where the current owners are celebrating their centenary of custodianship.

This year's Chairman's Award was presented to **Barry Haseltine** in recognition of his long service to the RCMG, holding office as a Trustee, Group Secretary and Yearbook Editor, demonstrating his true spirit of volunteering. Alongside these demanding committee roles, he has held the position of SE Branch Chairman continuously for more than 15 years.

Philip Eastell, our new Membership Secretary, seems to have got his feet truly under the table. He has revitalised our Garden Membership scheme, previously Corporate Membership, and judging by the numbers of gardens that are signing up, it seems to have captured the imagination. As a result we have a number of gardeners at the younger end of the age scale, which I believe will be invigorating for the Group.

We have been unable to make any Bursary awards for the past two years because there were no applications due to travel difficulties during the pandemic. It looks as though that may be changing. A recent application has resulted in us developing our relationship with the Royal Botanic Garden Edinburgh (RBGE), which will probably lead to us joining the Global Conservation Consortia (GCC). This initiative has been launched by Botanic Gardens Conservation International (BGCI) with the aim of mobilising a coordinated network of institutions and experts to collaboratively develop and implement comprehensive conservation strategies for priority threatened plant groups. The RGBE has indicated its interest in having all four of its National Botanic Gardens of Scotland accredited, where appropriate, under our Outstanding Garden Scheme.

DEFRA are consulting on a proposed ban on the sale of peat and peat containing products (products that wholly or partially include peat) in the retail sector. This, if implemented, would have a detrimental effect on the propagation by nurseries of some of our plants and also for those amateurs who grow them, since peat-free composts have yet to be shown as suitable replacements. In conjunction with other specialist groups we are continuing to give evidence to DEFRA and hopefully a solution satisfactory to all will be accomplished; based on previous experience I am less than optimistic.

Brexit seems to have come and gone with relatively little effect on our gardening activities although the various regulations relating to plant health and import/export continue to compromise our seed list offerings. However, our members have shown their resourcefulness in collecting seed for our list, which continues to be really popular and vibrant whereas it could so easily have disappeared.

Despite these apparent difficulties, overall I feel very positive about the Group's future and look forward to reporting more on that in 2023.

Graham Mills, Chairman

Editor for the Rhododendron, Camellia and Magnolia Group
Mary White

Commissioning Editors for the Group
David Millais, John Marston, Polly Cooke and Caroline Bell

Designed & Edited for the RHS by Marina Jordan-Rugg

Published in 2022 by the Royal Horticultural Society, 80 Vincent Square, London SW1P 2PE

ISBN 9 781911 666226

Printed by Short Run Press

Cover illustrations
Front cover: *Magnolia doltsopa* 'Silver Cloud' (Graham Mills); back cover (left): *Rhododendron aperantum* F26937 (Pink) (John McQuire); back cover (right): *Camellia chuangtsoensis* (Chip Lima)

RHS
Rhododendron, Camellia & Magnolia Group

Editorial

Mary White

Welcome all to your 2022 Yearbook. Thank you once again to our four commissioning editors John Marston, Polly Cooke, Caroline Bell and David Millais. If you have any subjects that you would like to write about for our 2023 Yearbook based around rhododendrons, camellias and magnolias they and I would love to hear from you. We are always on the lookout! You do not need to be a member to contribute, and there is no need to wait, we are 'all ears'. Thanks also to our generous authors, advertisers and regular contributors.

Once again our usual programme of shows for 2021 was disrupted so that as a group we were unable to hold any of our spring shows. To compensate for this The Centenary Cup Competition was once again held in photographic format. I feel very honoured to have won the overall competition with the photograph of *Rhododendron* 'Fortune', a plant my husband Roderick and I were given by a former member of the group, John Fox, 25 years ago when he moved to a smaller garden and us to a larger one. It was in splendid flower last year. You will have seen it in the Bulletin and photographs for the other winners feature in this Yearbook (pp112–116). This year, covid permitting, The Centenary Cup will be awarded to the winner of a physical show at Ramster Garden, Chiddingfold in May where our AGM will also be held.

Over the past year we have been able to get back to more of our usual pursuits, visiting gardens and friends. However, our very generous authors have still managed to find time to write some excellent articles. Olav Kalleberg shares his life with magnolias at 'Magnolia Heaven' with us (pp8–11) while Charles Williams VMH, after my plea for magnolia articles last year, runs us through the newest magnolia hybrids (pp43–52). Maurice Foster VMH talks about the unresolved question of *Magnolia sinensis* and its correct naming (pp26–29)and Brigitte Wachsmuth gives us the historical origins, circumstances and numerous names of *Camellia* 'Vergine di Collebeato' (pp37–42). Erland Ejder enlightens us about *Magnolia sinostellata*, its worthiness as a small magnolia for the garden and its fight for habitat alongside human progress and the efforts of the Botanic Gardens Conservation International to help (pp70–77). Similarly, Patrick Thompson talks about his conservation work in Alabama to sustain deciduous azaleas in their fight for survival in an ever-changing climate and world (pp102–111). Abbie Jury shows us new ways to prune and shape camellias and the changes she and her husband Mark have made in growing species and small-flowered camellias in response to camellia petal blight, which spoils the large-flowered types all too readily (pp18–25). Jim Stephens shares his notes from a camellia volunteer at Mount Edgcumbe with some helpful pruning advice and his quest to correctly label all the camellias there – no mean feat (pp92–101)! Everard Daniel and Joanne Ryan investigate the possible origin and history of the enormous specimen of *Rhododendron falconeri* at Leith Hill Place in Surrey (pp12–17) and John Hammond gives us a detailed story about the early history of hybridising rhododendrons in North Yorkshire and the development of the rhododendron garden at Harewood House (pp78–91). Audrey Tam tells us of John Gault's *Rhododendron maximum* 'Red Max' (pp53–55) in response to an article that they both read in the *American Rhododendron Society Journal* last year by Donald Hyatt, and Brenda Litchfield recounts her visits to The Palm Valley Nursery Company, the nursery responsible for breeding many new "ever-blooming" camellias, a few of which are slowly becoming available to buy in the UK (pp56–69).

The late Barry Starling AOH also sent me an article (pp30–36) describing some more alpine rhododendrons in response to John Good's article in last year's edition. I was particularly happy to receive it; I had not requested Barry to write anything for the Yearbook as he so generously contributed to the Bulletin on a regular basis. It is the last article he wrote for us; I was not expecting anything from him and was delighted to receive it, typed on his typewriter and sent with a box of slides. It arrived on a very dark, wet, Saturday in January. It certainly made my weekend. The end of an era, the group will miss him very much, as will the Alpine Garden Society to name but two. He will be remembered with a detailed article in our 2023 Yearbook to commemorate his enormous contribution to horticulture in so many ways. A short appreciation was included in the March Bulletin to announce his death. Jens Birck will also be commemorated with a much larger piece in our 2023 Yearbook, the authors also felt that a short appreciation could not do him justice for his extensive rhododendron hybridising work carried out over many years. Sadly, appreciations are always needed in our Yearbook as we seem to have had a wealth of great names in the world of rhododendrons, camellias and magnolias. This year Harold Eldon Greer is remembered by John Hammond and Gordon Wylie (pp120–121).

Our usual RHS Awards were conducted, once again with the exception of the Rothschild Challenge Cup, given the lack of spring shows. We hope to be able to award this one once again next year. Congratulations go to the recipients of all the other awards (pp117–119).

The International Rhododendron Registrar (pp122–127) and the International Magnolia Registrar (pp128–129) have both been busy with new registrations over the past year as has the International Camellia Registrar in particular. More than 250 new camellias were registered

Editor Mary White (far right) **with Pam and Barry Starling in their garden in 2019** *photo:* **Roderick White**

mostly from China he tells me. I have been lucky enough to have received permission from the International Camellia Society to reprint their recent new European introductions (p130–133). My thanks go to the Editor, Frieda Delvaux and Dr Gianmario Motta the ICS President for this.

I write this just after storm Eunice, a rather devastating blast in February 2022 with Finlay hot on her heels. Similarly, storms Arwen and Barra, which struck in November and December 2021, were other very destructive forces. Scotland, Ireland and northern England seemed to endure a storm a week during the winter, not all of them named of course. All of these have changed many of our favourite rhododendron, camellia and magnolia gardens forever with the loss of many large trees and ancient specimens; indeed some gardens may not re-open to the public until 2023. On the face of it this is a disaster but I am sure that once all the clearing up and taking stock has happened, like all of us, the gardeners will have ten more new plants to fill each space – just which ones to choose from all those new introductions? A happy dilemma for us all.

Happy gardening in 2022.

Mary White, Editor

My life with magnolias at Magnolia Heaven, Norway

Olav Kalleberg

Magnolia Heaven, Sira, south-western Norway – *all photographs:* **Olav Kalleberg**

For about 40 years now I have been growing magnolias at Sira in south-western Norway. I started by planting lots of trees such as *Robinia*, *Sciadopitys verticillata* cultivars and many different conifers before Mr. Lennarth Jonsson of Sweden suggested planting magnolias.

In Sweden, magnolias had been grown and trialled for a long time so I thought: Why not in Norway? Norway is influenced by the waters of the Gulf Stream, so the climate is relatively mild where I live.

My villa garden is about 1,500 square metres and it was soon too small for me so I bought more land: 1.3 hectares (3.2 acres) to be exact. I named the area Magnolia Heaven because it is situated near the local church and because it had long been my dream to plant magnolias. I followed my dream.

I also made a Pinetum close to the collections of magnolias where I planted robinias, cytisus, laburnums and so on to provide nitrogen to the sandy soil without using artificial fertiliser. The collection is growing on a moraine with perfect drainage.

The precipitation (average/year) is 1800mm (70in) and the average temperature a year: 6.5C. Extreme temperatures are from -20C to +34C. The snow and rain often come and go during the winter and deep frost in the soil may be a problem because snow is so unpredictable in our part of Norway. Last winter there was frost in the soil for six months.

I have taken meteorological observations for many years with a special emphasis on temperatures. There is a National Meteorological station close to my property

Magnolia sieboldii 'Genesis' x M. virginiana

that measures the local precipitation.

The very first magnolia I planted was a *Magnolia sieboldii* after I had observed a 5m tall plant of it growing near the local train station; its beautiful flowers fascinated me.

After that, I imported many small magnolias from Otto Eisenhut's nursery in Ticino, Switzerland because there were very few magnolias in Norwegian nurseries, these were mainly *Magnolia stellata, M. kobus, M.* 'Susan' and also *M. × soulangeana*, which is not hardy at my place. Only *M. × soulangeana* 'Sundew' has survived since the mid-eighties here. It is one of Amos Pickard's cultivars.

As I planted more magnolias I bought lots of books about them. I corresponded with many experts and propagators such as August E. Kehr, John Gallagher, Neil Treseder, Phil Savage, Richard Figlar, Dennis Ledvina, Wim Rutten, Sir Peter Smithers, Carl Ferris Miller, Tommy Ahnby, Tor Nitzelius, Pat McCracken, Richard Jaynes, Harold Greer, Song Sparrow Nursery and Quakin' Grass Nursery.

I have also provided several nurseries abroad with grafting material. For many years I corresponded with the late Dr August E. Kehr writing of our shared experiences. 'Augie' was a kind and generous man and I miss him.

I also corresponded with the late Dr Frank Galyon who I remember having wonderful handwriting as did the late Carl Ferris Miller who wrote on a thin rice paper. The latter telephoned me from Arboretum Chollipo when he had sent some plants to me. I was honoured. I remember his deep voice.

I remember reading a very interesting and long scientific article about magnolias (a monograph) written by Karl Evert Flinck from Sweden. He was a "magnoliauru" (uru means big or expert) in Sweden at that time, and he almost reached the age of 100.

I collaborated with Tommy Ahnby by sending seeds of magnolia crosses made by the late Dennis Ledvina to him. Dennis shared seeds with several "magnolia nuts" and I was one of them.

Tommy raised the seedlings, which I then purchased from him at a fair price as I had helped him with obtaining seeds and grafting material. He still runs his Gullmarsfjordens Plantskola wholesale nursery in Sweden. Tommy obtained a phytosanitary certificate, which enabled him to send plants to me at Rammegård in Norway. He had "hagedager" (open garden days) there.

In 1988 I raised a plant from seeds I obtained from Gothenburg Botanical Garden in Sweden, which bloomed for the first time in 1995. I believe that it's the only one of the cross *M. obovata × M. sieboldii* and I named it after my long-suffering wife: *M. × wieseneri* 'Aashild Kalleberg'. The reverse cross, *M. × wieseneri* 'Swede Made' (*M. sieboldii × M. obovata*) was named by Stefan Mattson.

From the USA I had to import bare-rooted plants and I lost quite a few when they took too long to reach me but I still managed to obtain several goodies from Pat McCracken before most collectors in Europe. I also imported from Song Sparrow Nursery, which has now closed but they specialised in magnolias on their own roots, which I firmly believe give the best results.

I have layered many grafted magnolias and some have layered themselves. Several of

Magnolia 'Dennis Ledvina'

Magnolia x *weiseneri* 'Swede Made'

Dennis Ledvina's crosses are easy to root.

For several years, I imported magnolias from Wim Rutten in the Netherlands and after his early death I continued to import them from Job Vergeldt who took over his business.

In Germany, Michael Gottschalk helped me to obtain plants and shared information about availability. He runs Lunaplant nursery and made a cross of *M.* 'Black Tulip' × *M. liliiflora* 'Holland Red', which he named after me: *M.* 'Olav Kalleberg' thereby fulfilling my dream of a hardier *M.* 'Black Tulip'. It performs much better than 'Black Tulip' in our climate. The mother plant growing in my garden is now 15 years old.

It is difficult to import plants to Norway and very often the foreign nursery writes on its website; "We do not ship plants to Norway"! A phytosanitary certificate is a must and therefore it is expensive to import plants here.

I am moderator of the Facebook group Magnolia Heaven. We have more than 2,000 members and many of them are experts on magnolias but there are also many amateurs.

I have been responsible for naming the following magnolias: *M.* 'Dennis Ledvina', *M.* 'Gullmarsfjord', *M.* 'Tommy's Fragrant Heaven', *M. sieboldii* 'Reinan', *M. kobus* 'Octopus', *M. sieboldii* 'Pride of Norway', *M. sieboldii* 'Min Pyong-gal' (Mr Carl Ferris Miller's Korean name); and of course, *M.* × *wieseneri* 'Aashild Kalleberg'. The Norwegian letter "Å" is replaced with "Aa".

I have also lost many plants for several reasons: drought, poor plants or roots, deer, frost and heavy snow. It is impossible to get irrigation going at Magnolia Heaven and the soil is not very deep. Some magnolias are too tender to grow, such as *M. grandiflora*, and some have too short a growing season at Magnolia Heaven to harden off properly before winter comes.

I do not use fertiliser and never remove fallen leaves or dead grass from the ground.

The pH of the soil is 5 and so rhododendrons and *Sciadopitys verticillata* (umbrella pine) are planted among the magnolias. *Robinia* × *ambigua* 'Decaisneana' has nice flowers and long thorns and suckers appear among the plantings.

Newly planted magnolias must not compete with grass although it works well when the plants are more mature. Old leaves and other organic material are used as mulches around the trunks during the winter.

The magnolias may be injured by late

Magnolia x *weiseneri* '**Aashild Kalleberg**' (top left);
M. 'Olav Kalleberg' (left); **M. *sieboldii* 'Harold
Epstein'** (top right); **Magnolia Heaven
Conservatory** (above)

spring frost but I have magnolias that are summer bloomers and others have a solid rebloom late in the season. One season *M. × wieseneri* bloomed in the first week of November. The earliest time the first magnolias flowered in one season was late in March.

Magnolia Heaven is at 80m above sea level and sheltered from cold northern and northeastern winds by a rock and a hill. Blowing from other directions the winds are often strong but the magnolias have not been seriously damaged although wet, heavy snow may be a problem.

My 15 square metre conservatory is fully insulated and I have electricity there. It's the perfect place to read and rest inside after having worked on the collection, enjoying a panoramic view of the beautiful landscape.

• Search 'Olav Kalleberg's beautiful garden' on YouTube for a drone video of my collection.

Olav Kalleberg *is a Magnolia specialist and breeder who has introduced many well-known magnolia hybrids over the years.*

A fabulous and historic rhododendron in Surrey

Joanne Ryan and Everard Daniel

Rhododendron falconeri at Leith Hill – *photo:* **Mike Timberlake**

Taking a walk round the National Trust's Rhododendron Wood at Leith Hill Place, we were both stopped in our tracks by one of the finest rhododendrons in south east England. It's a stupendously beautiful plant of *Rhododendron falconeri*, perfectly sited on the slopes of a sheltered south-facing gully. The big bold leaves make it a stunning architectural foliage plant all year, never mind the flowers. In August 2021 it was measured at 10m high with the largest stem having a girth of 1.08m and the base having a girth of 3.46m measured 20cm from ground level. It is said to be the largest example of its kind in the south east of England.

Moreover, this seems to be an historic plant with a fascinating story, as it is mentioned in the Darwin correspondence. On 28 April 1864 Emma Darwin, Charles' wife, ends a letter discussing family matters with Sir Joseph Hooker with these exciting words:
"We have just received a blossom of Rhod Falconeri which has flowered in the open air at my brothers on Leith Hill Surrey. This day is a fortnight since he has had any sickness. With my love to Mrs Hooker yours very truly E.D."

Some background

Sir Joseph Hooker was, perhaps, the most eminent botanist of Victorian Britain and was

Rhododendron falconeri – photo: **Everard Daniel**   *R. falconeri – photo:* **Joanne Ryan/National Trust**

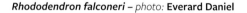

one of the closest and most supportive friends that Charles Darwin had. In 1855 he became Assistant Director of the Royal Botanic Gardens, Kew, and in 1865 Hooker succeeded his father as Director, a post that he held for 20 years. He interspersed work at Kew with foreign exploration and collecting. His journeys to Palestine, Morocco and the United States all produced valuable information and specimens for Kew. All these expeditions and collections are recorded in the impressive list of books he published. Of most relevance here are the years 1847–1850 that he spent in India and his collecting trip into Sikkim.

Rhododendron falconeri was one of the rhododendrons collected during his Himalayan travels and described in his *Rhododendrons of Sikkim-Himalaya*. He mentioned the species several times in his "Himalayan journals" noting that the "30ft tall tree" was "in point of foliage the most superb of all the Himalayan species".

Hooker is credited with introducing many rhododendron species to Western collections.

To the south of Dorking, the Lower Greensand rises up to form Leith Hill, which with its tower, built in 1765, forms the highest point in south east England. Leith Hill Place is on the southern slopes, with a great view over the Weald. It was owned by Josiah Wedgwood III (of the illustrious pottery family); he and Charles Darwin were cousins and married each other's sisters, Emma and Caroline respectively. Hence Emma Darwin referring to Wedgwood as her brother and it was Caroline

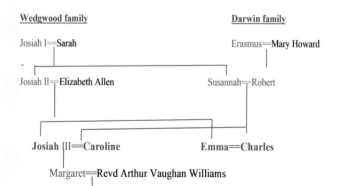

Simplified Family Tree

Wedgwood family   Darwin family

Josiah I==Sarah   Erasmus==Mary Howard

Josiah II==Elizabeth Allen   Susannah==Robert

Josiah III==Caroline   Emma==Charles

Margaret==Revd Arthur Vaughan Williams

Ralph Vaughan Williams

Rhododendron Wood, Leith Hill Place

Rhododendron augustinii, Leith Hill Place
– *photos:* **Joanne Ryan/National Trust**

Rhododendron Wood, Leith Hill Place

A few massive original plantings of *Sequoiadendron giganteum* and several huge old plants of *Rhododendron* Smithii Group, *R.* 'Cunningham's Blush', *R.* 'Ivery's Scarlet', *R.* 'Cynthia' and *R.* 'Lady Eleanor Cathcart' remain as well as all sorts of other interesting things, many of which are tucked away but are beginning to reveal themselves as the National Trust carries out more work to understand Caroline's Rhododendron Wood. The *R. augustinii* are a very good, blue clone. There is also a very good collection of old Ghent azaleas, which are likely to be from a second wave of planting. They are estimated to be in excess of 100–120 years old.

Little primary evidence has been found so far of Caroline and Josiah's time at Leith Hill Place, what their lives were like there and how they spent their time. One source states that they brought with them a well-respected gardener from Staffordshire, so this must mean they wanted to make a garden and the landscape around their house was important to them.

The Rhododendron Wood today has at its core and throughout many examples of old hardy hybrids, which are substantial, established specimens and may well date back to Caroline's period of influence. Most of these have *R. arboreum* in their parentage and so are massive and majestic plants formed of multi stems and layers, creating bold focal points of form and colour. *R.* Smithii Group is a *R. ponticum × arboreum* hybrid made first in the 1830s but repeated many times since, which has led to variations in spotting of the flowers and indumentum on the leaves, but habit and effect are fairly constant. Several examples of this group are growing in the woodland, appear healthy and still flower well. There is also evidence that they were planting new and exciting species in the woodland. Within a few years of them moving to Leith Hill Place, Hooker brought back several new species of *Rhododendron* from Sikkim. This caused great excitement in the horticultural world and seeds and plants were sent out far and wide.

Back to *Rhododendron falconeri*

So is this the plant in the letter? We do know that Darwin visited his sister and brother-in-law often and it seems he did make rhododendron observations in the woodland because there are letters written by him from Leith Hill Place to Hooker, with

R. falconeri close-up of flower

Leaf size, shape and thick indumentum of *R. falconeri* at Leith Hill

Magnificent trunk of *R. falconeri* at Leith Hill Place – *photos:* **Joanne Ryan/National Trust**

rhododendrons as the subject. They correspond about rhododendron flower morphology and there is evidence that he sent specimens from Leith Hill Place for identification to Hooker, namely *R. glaucum* (today considered as *R. glaucophyllum*). We feel that the wonderful old specimen of *R. falconeri* still growing strong in the woodland and another specimen nearby are almost certainly from the original Hooker introduction batch. Alas having looked at the original 'plants outwards' books at Kew, there is no evidence to confirm this, no listing of material going directly to the Wedgwoods or Leith Hill Place. Darwin received 12 Sikkim rhododendrons on 2 April 1855, however their species are unfortunately not listed and there are no records where these were planted. So could this *R. falconeri* have been one of Darwin's 12? The Kew records show that in total 16 *R. falconeri* were recorded as being distributed from Kew.

Flower colour, blotches, size and shape of the Leith Hill Place *R. falconeri* – *photo:* Joanne Ryan/National Trust

The Darwins lived at Down House near Bromley in Kent, on top of the North Downs. The former head gardener there says they have no records of *R. falconeri* ever growing there, and don't have many rhododendrons now. Could Darwin have given some of his 12 Sikkim rhododendrons to his sister for the Rhododendron Wood planting? We think this could well be possible, indeed very likely. If this species of rhododendron had some significance to Darwin and Caroline then that would explain why it was mentioned in the letter that Emma Darwin sent to Hooker in 1864, and why a bloom was sent to Darwin in the first place. Circumstantial but pretty conclusive that this is indeed the very plant.

Some botany
Joanne has recorded voucher notes and data for the *R. falconeri*:

One plant, a magnificent and colossal specimen, branching low down into nine trunks, the largest 120cm girth at waist height. Branchlets densely tomentose with brownish

hairs. Bark golden brown and flaking. Approximately 8–10m tall.

One of the things that stands out is the number of stamens and the number of flowers per truss. Compared to general species accounts, this specimen seems to have more stamens : 16, 16, 17, 17, 16, 16, 18, 16, 16, 20, 18 and far more flowers per truss : 39, 31, 30, 26, 28, 33, 32, 29, 33, 38. Counting the stamens in 10 different flowers on 10 different trusses, and number of flowers on 10 different trusses, gives some sense of the average.

Perhaps this is a variation within a species found in an old seed-grown specimen compared with current clonal specimens. Compare with Davidian who says 12–20 flowers per truss, stamens 12–16. Perhaps older specimens have more flowers and stamens? It would be interesting to hear from members and their observations about older plants.

More subsequent history
One of Josiah and Caroline's grandsons grew up to be one of the finest English composers, Ralph Vaughan Williams. His wonderful music includes nine symphonies, choral works large and small, film music (Scott of the Antarctic) and so much else. He is perhaps best known for the majestic, other-worldly Tallis Fantasia, also the Fantasia on Greensleeves and The Lark Ascending, which regularly tops the Classic FM chart. He founded the Leith Hill Festival for local choirs to compete at, still held annually in Dorking.

He was born in Down Ampney where his father was the vicar (hence the name of one of his finest hymn tunes). However, his father died young and his mother Margaret (nee Wedgwood) brought the family to live with her parents at Leith Hill Place. So young Ralph would have been familiar with great-uncle Charles Darwin and his earthworm experiments on the lawn there. It is said that when he asked about evolution, he was told "Well God created the World in seven days, but Uncle Charles thinks it took rather longer".

In 1944, Ralph inherited the property and gave it to the National Trust. It is only recently that the restoration of the house has started and enabled it to be opened up, being used for various crafts and activities and to tell us about this extraordinary family.

Conclusions

Leith Hill Place, with its lovely position, woods, views and sandy soil is the ideal setting for a very informal woodland garden full of treasures. The crowning glory is undoubtably the stunning specimen of *R. falconeri*; it is awesome in the true sense of the word. Beautiful and colossal, it was planted in a brilliantly thoughtful position on a gentle sheltered slope, which was clearly chosen with an eye to the future, to perhaps be passed and admired when Caroline took one of her regular walks.

The National Trust has propagated this important specimen at its Plant Conservation Centre and, in time, young plants will be distributed to be planted in other gardens. When we go to Leith Hill, whether it is flowering or not, we have to go for a gaze – it has truly got under our skin. As the saying goes "Worth a journey".

Herbarium voucher sheet preparation and flower parts in detail
– *photos:* **Joanne Ryan/National Trust**

ACKNOWLEDGEMENTS

Joanne wishes to thank Jim Inskip, Polly and Barry Cooke and Andy Fly for their help and enthusiasm.
Data reproduced with permission of the National Trust.

REFERENCES

Darwin Correspondence Project, 'Letter no. 4473', accessed on 25 February 2021, www.darwinproject.ac.uk/letter/DCP-LETT-4473.xml
Hooker, J D *The Rhododendrons of Sikkim-Himalaya*, 3 parts, 1849–1851 and modern facsimile, Kew Publishing, RBG Kew.
Personal correspondence with Rowan Blaik former Head Gardener, Down House.
Wedgwood, B and H, *The Wedgwood Circle 1730–1897*, Studio Vista, 1980.

Joanne Ryan *is a Horticultural Botanist in the National Trust Plant Conservation Team.*

Everard Daniel *is a long-time member of the South East branch of the group with a special interest in camellias, rhododendron hybrids, magnolias and hydrangeas.*

New directions with camellias

Abbie Jury

I married into a camellia family. Both Les and Felix Jury were recognised in their day as making significant contributions to the camellia world with their new cultivars. Both worked with *Camellia japonica* and hybrids to create plants that were self-grooming (dropping spent flowers rather than having them hang onto the bush) and breeding out the tendency for stamens to turn black as blooms aged. Hugely popular in New Zealand, camellias ranked second only to roses in sales figures.

My own mother was not as keen. True, she described a young plant of Felix's

C. sasanqua 'Crimson King' with the open, graceful form many sasanquas have as they mature – *all photographs:* **Abbie Jury**

C. × williamsii 'Rose Bouquet' as being like growing an herbaceous peony in a climate that did not favour the growing of peonies at all, but it was clear she saw it as second best. Once, memorably, she declared that the trouble with camellias was that they were all red, white or pink blobs with shiny green foliage. With experience, I now realise she was only thinking of *C. japonica* and related hybrids. I do not think she ever met the species or had anything to do with *C. sasanqua*.

We have a large garden with camellias used in a variety of situations. I have never counted them but they will be in the hundreds, not the tens. When Mark started plant breeding, he followed in the footsteps of his father and his uncle and chose camellias first. They are right at home in our climate so we have camellias as feature plants, background plants, hedges both informal and clipped, windbreaks and as a backbone plant repeated through the garden.

The arrival of camellia petal blight – *Ciborinia camelliae* – was nothing short of devastating and led to a change of approach with our camellias. Our massed displays of *C. reticulata*, *C. japonica* and hybrids blooming in winter and spring disappeared as petal blight took hold and now they are just a memory. Petal blight is common throughout the world. Is it only Australia that remains free from it? It took a trip to the International Camellia Congress in southern China in 2016 for us to realise that our particular climatic conditions mean that the impact of blight here is arguably at the very worst end of the scale. We are humid and mild with regular

Camellia minutiflora **shrub** (above) **and close-up** (above right)

rainfall and plenty of wind to spread spores far and wide – ideal conditions for any fungal ailment. In the drier conditions of China, it was nowhere near as big a problem and talking to growers from around the world, they do not suffer the same level of impact as we do.

In our particular location, it is bad enough now for me to say that we have not and would not plant a *C. japonica*, a large-flowered hybrid or a *C. reticulata*. There is no point. Flowering has become sparse and all that early breeding for plants that are self-grooming does not work for these vulnerable camellias. The display is now either pale brown, blighted blooms or blooms in the process of being blighted with just a few lovely flowers to remind us of times past.

All is not lost, but we have done a serious re-think. Fortunately, Mark had always been interested in miniature-flowered camellias with a strong personal preference for the simplicity of singles and semi-doubles. They mass flower and each bloom only lasts a couple of days so they fall before blight takes hold. We also like the species and had already set out to build a collection of those available

in this country. Some of the species bring in a wider range of growth habits and foliage than is seen in commercial camellias. In fact, some do not even look like camellias as most people know them. We are so besotted with little *C. minutiflora* that we have several in the garden; what came to us as *C. puniceiflora* does not look like a camellia at all and only aficionados would identify the pink-flowered form of *C. sinensis* and the assorted yellow species we have as camellias.

We also have a good representation of autumn-flowering varieties from the *C. sasanqua* group, which are not affected by blight. In the days when the large-flowered *C. japonica* types were favoured, with a preference for the perfection of formal doubles like 'Dreamboat' and scores of others, the attitude to *C. sasanqua* was a bit dismissive. They lack the solid petal texture and defined form in their blooms and are slower to establish, as nursery plants at least. In New Zealand, they were largely seen as utility hedging, best in white and even better in *C. sasanqua* 'Setsugekka'. The white 'Setsugekka' hedge became a cliché.

Tastes can change. Now we appreciate the *C. sasanqua* cultivars for their mass display in autumn through to early winter, preferring that looser flower structure and simplicity. Added to that, as mature plants, most have a naturally graceful form that is easy to tidy up and enhance to create a feature plant even when not in bloom. Shapes are important all year round and shapes with good, healthy foliage that are also hardy, reliable and low maintenance are not to be disdained.

We give a lot more thought to our camellia plants these days. Many are invaluable for shelter and wind breaks. Flowers are a bonus. But not every camellia plant is valuable. If they are not flowering at all well, are not pleasing to the eye as a shrub and are not filling a useful purpose, we have no qualms about removing them. All these plants used to at least fulfil one of those functions – that of mass flowering.

We do a lot of what we call lifting and limbing here. In a mature garden, raising the canopy and letting in light is ongoing. What sets lifting and limbing apart from simple pruning is that it is more focused on making the most of the natural shape of the mature plant. Mark is the master of this but my skills are improving. More time is spent standing and looking, then tracing where branches go, than actually cutting. There is much going up and down the ladder. It is very satisfying to

Lifting and Limbing – finding the natural shape of the plant and highlighting it as with *Camellia* **'Tiny Princess'** (above left) **and C. × williamsii 'Dreamboat'** (above)

find the pleasing forms within a plant and to highlight the shape by removing extraneous growth. Added to that, it is a one-off activity that just needs a bit of occasional maintenance in future years. It is possible to remove a large amount without a plant looking massacred, as long as clean cuts close to the trunk or branch are made.

Our garden is very light on ornamentation. We do not go in for sculptures, statuary, pots or a plethora of trellises and archways, preferring to use key plants as focal points, along with natural vistas. Mark's cloud-pruned camellias are particularly fetching. He started on *Camellia sasanqua* 'Mine-no-yuki (sasanqua)', which was so huge that its weeping growth was blocking a pathway. The initial shaping took him several days climbing up and down the ladder, which was hard on his knees. He must have removed well over half the jumbled plant but found the most pleasing shape beneath. We keep it clipped to flat-topped cloud shapes. It only needs trimming once a year to maintain that form and now it is a simple job that takes a couple of hours with hedge clippers. 'Mine-no-yuki (sasanqua)' is not good in bloom here. We get

Cloud-pruned 'Mine-no-yuki (sasanqua)'

Cloud-pruned 'Elfin Rose'

a few days of pristine white blooms before they become weather damaged; from then on we get a display of brown and white flowers. As a clipped, evergreen shrub it makes a splendid feature all year round.

I differentiate between clipping and pruning. Pruning is done with a pruning saw and secateurs; clipping is carried out with trimmers, be they hand-held hedge clippers or motorised trimming blades. Good pruning is a higher grade skill because the aim is to get into the plant and shape it without the work being visible – an older colleague used to call it 'blind pruning'. Hacking is bad pruning.

We do not clip many plants – ours is not a garden modelled on the clipped and corseted Italian genre – but we have a few that we like to use as punctuation points in the garden. Inside our entrance, we have a small grouping of camellias that we clip tightly once a year. The shape of each has been entirely determined by exaggerating their natural growth habits. So *C. gauchowensis* is a plump, rounded pillar, *C. puniceiflora* a three tier cake-stand and the somewhat insignificant *C. trichoclada* is a flat plinth. They are backed by the cloud-pruned *C.* × *hiemalis* 'Elfin Rose'.

The problem with clipping is that it cuts every single outside leaf, which then turns brown on the cut edge. This does not matter

when it is done on plants with very small leaves and it is not generally a problem on the *C. sasanqua* cultivars which have a somewhat softer leaf. It matters a great deal if the clipping candidate has the tough, shiny, leathery leaves common to the *C. japonica* types. I drive past a clipped white *C. japonica* hedge from time to time and it simply looks awful when it has been freshly cut. I wonder if the owners went to buy the aforementioned 'Setsugekka' (which would have been much more successful) but the garden centre had sold out, so talked them into a white japonica

Clipped camellias (left to right) **C. 'Elfin Rose',
C. puniceiflora, C. gauchowensis with C. trichoclada**
(foreground)**. All are clipped once a year**

21

Our preferred hedging options (left to right)
C. microphylla, 'Fairy Blush' and *C. transnokoensis*

Camellia 'Fairy Blush' as a clipped hedge

instead? It was not a good choice. Keep your clippers away from *C. japonica* varieties is my advice; reach for the secateurs instead and forget any ideas of tight-clipped shapes.

We have camellia hedges ourselves, but all are small-leafed varieties that clip tightly to make a dense barrier over time and they then look sharp-edged and smart. We also select camellia varieties for small single flowers that drop cleanly and break down quickly, thereby avoiding the brown sludge that large, heavy-textured flowers can create when they fall. The three camellias we have used for hedging are 'Fairy Blush', *C. transnokoenis* and *C. microphylla*. 'Fairy Blush' is our first choice where we want dense hedges to around 1.5 or 1.8m high. It is a *C. lutchuensis* hybrid, the first camellia Mark ever named and the one that remains our all-time favourite with its exceptionally long flowering season. Unlike its scented parent, it is fully tolerant of sun and open conditions (*C. lutchuensis* is inclined to yellowing foliage in full sun), very free flowering and, en masse, it exudes a delightful scent on warmer, sunny days.

We have never grown much *Buxus* hedging here but when the threat of box blight loomed (mercifully, it has still not reached us and we do not have the box caterpillar in New Zealand), Mark took the opportunity to rip out a couple of hedges and replace them with *C. transnokoensis*. I think the blight might have been an excuse really, because the main reason was that he thinks hedges should be more than green walls; they should also contribute to the eco-system and plants that flower and attract bees and butterflies do more than just act as a visual divider. *C. transnokoensis* has excellent small foliage and tiny white blooms but its flowering season is much shorter than 'Fairy Blush' and it is taking longer to become dense in its growth.

C. microphylla has an even shorter season in bloom and flowers in late autumn for us, but we selected it less for its white, starry blooms and more for its very compact habit and small leaves, which lends it to tighter clipping. We

Camellia yuhsienensis with *Magnolia* × 'Fairy White' (above). **It is possible to remove a lot of the plant without it looking as though it has been brutally attacked if pruning is considered and careful – shaping and reducing** *C. yuhsienensis* (below and inset)

C. microphylla **is kept low as an undulating wave hedge, between 30 and 70cm high**

wanted low, undulating hedges in the area we call the Wave Garden. It is taking some time to grow and clip into the tight growth we want, particularly because the plants Mark had raised from both cuttings and seed languished, unloved, in pots in the nursery for longer than they should have. It took us a while to plan and then plant the garden they were destined to grace. Healthier plants would have taken off faster but we can see it will work exactly as planned.

When it comes to tight clipping, timing is important. We tend to clip hard in early to mid-spring, just as new growth is being made. If it gets left later, flower buds will have set and clipping will be at the expense of next season's flowering. Sometimes we get to the *C. sasanqua* plants earlier; in our relatively mild climate, we have more latitude and can garden through winter without risk. We only clip once but we are not worried by the softer,

23

woolly look that develops as the seasons progress. If you want a sharper look, do a hard spring clip, then follow up in summer with a light prune to tidy the wayward fresh growths.

Overall, we do more pruning than clipping and that is aimed at keeping key plants from growing to their full potential. Essentially, we are trying to contain them to a certain size. We have used the lesser-known species, *C. yuhsienensis*, as punctuation points adding winter interest along the summer gardens. We love its open, starry blooms, which are lightly scented and reminiscent of a michelia as well as the heavy-textured foliage that many people fail to identify as a camellia. It is not self-grooming and it is one of the few camellias I am willing to go through and brush off spent blooms – a sign of how much it pleases me. Left to its own devices, it will reach 2.5 to 3m high by 2m wide in our conditions, getting somewhat more open as it grows. I keep the plants to around 1.6m high and 1m wide with a single, perfectly straightforward annual prune with secateurs and sometimes a handsaw. Each plant is reviewed individually

A top-worked hybrid of Mark's we named 'Pearly Cascade', which is unlikely to still be in cultivation. While the flower is not special, the slow, spreading growth habit kept it small and made it an ideal candidate for training into a feature plant

as I work out which branches I want to take out entirely and which ones I just want to shorten. It sounds more onerous than it is in practice but my aim is always that the pruning should not be visible to other people's eyes.

We have a few high-worked standard camellias, grafted a metre or so up a single, strong trunk. These are not easy to propagate and therefore not widely available commercially here, if at all these days. Our plants date back to when we still had a plant nursery and specialised in unusual options. The weepers are just left to weep. These are 'Quintessence' and one that came to us as 'Nuccio's Pink Cascade' but I cannot find that name online. I scrapped all the weeping 'Sweet Emily Kate' specimens because the exceptionally pretty flower did not atone for the dreadful yellowed foliage.

Our other standards are slow-growing hybrids from Mark's breeding programme that are not commercially available. Their natural characteristics of being both slow and dense in growth make them easy to maintain. Trying to create standards from stronger-growing varieties would mean a whole lot more work fighting nature to keep the desired shape.

A top-worked (high-grafted) weeper, which came to us as 'Nuccio's Pink Cascade' but that may not be an accurate name

Eight camellias have been retained in our sunken garden as clipped and shaped character plants together with two dwarf maples

Mark is not a lollipop or pompom man. He likes these camellias clipped to low, flattened domes – mushroom shapes, he calls them, or maybe umbrellas. An annual clip or prune is sufficient to keep these as statement plants.

I have never gone in for espalier, myself. I am not so keen on that level of extended fiddle-faddling but I admire a well-established espalier of *C.* × *hiemalis* 'Elfin Rose' in a garden down the road. It has been trained on a readymade trellis fan and is kept cut to make a dense screen that is only about 30cm deep.

In days gone by, I used to keep a small collection of trained and clipped camellias in large containers to move around to particular locations. Each one was treated differently to emphasise individual characteristics. I planted them out or gave them away because I decided that, in a garden as large as ours, having large plants in pots that needed regular watering, feeding, repotting and root pruning was too much work. I prefer to work on plants already growing in the ground but the container

approach may work in other situations.

When we removed the garden beds around the top of the sunken garden, we retained the eight camellias and two dwarf maples as clipped and shaped character plants.

We used to view camellias as a low-maintenance, undemanding but top-performing utility plant in our garden. That changed with petal blight. Now their roles have changed. We treat each plant individually and give them a lot more attention, but that is what makes gardening interesting for us. We would not be without them. It may be putting a brave face on it, but I am not sure I miss those days when they were largely big blobs of white, pink or red on shiny green foliage. Times change and we just change our gardening ways to meet the new situation.

Abbie Jury *is a gardener and garden writer. With her husband, magnolia breeder Mark Jury, she gardens at Tikorangi in Taranaki, on the west coast of New Zealand's North Island.*

The unresolved question of *Magnolia sinensis*

Maurice Foster

Type specimens
Magnolia sinensis –
The Herbarium of the
Arnold Arboretum of
Harvard University

The Wilson introduction

Ernest Wilson discovered what eventually became known as *Magnolia sinensis* during his 1908 expedition for the Arnold Arboretum, under his number W1422. He described it as "not uncommon in the moist woods and thickets of north western Szechuan" but only collected the type specimens in one location: between 2,000–2,600m near Wenchuan-hsien in June and September of 1908. He described it both as "a handsome flowering shrub" and "always a shrub of straggling habit".

In 1913 Rehder and Wilson published it as *Magnolia globosa* var. *sinensis*. Subsequently in 1926 Wilson suggested it should be placed within *M. globosa*, but three years earlier in 1923 Dr Otto Stapf had raised it to species level as *M. sinensis*. It went on to be accepted as a species by most authorities and authors until in 1976 Dr Stephen Spongberg treated it as a subspecies of *M. sieboldii*. Some follow this treatment, while others maintain it as a species.

The Spongberg revision

Dr Spongberg reached his decision by comparing it with a specimen of *M. sieboldii* growing in Martha's Vineyard in Massachusetts, concluding that the two could not be separated. "The flowering specimens of these two collections could well have come from a single gathering".

On further examination of a number of plants of both wild and cultivated origin, differences were noted that distinguished the two taxa. He differentiated *M. sinensis* as a subspecies of *M. sieboldii* on the basis of a number of characters – the young twigs are tomentose with yellowish or rufous hairs; it has occasionally larger leaf blades, broadly obovate to suborbicular; longer petioles, up to 6cm rather than the 1–3cm of the type; the lower leaf surface has crinkled or curled hairs; and the stipule scars reach more than half the length of the petiole.

Dr Spongberg explained these differences

as likely flowing from the disjunct situation of *M. sinensis*, which had become morphologically differentiated as a result of geographical isolation. However, although essentially a Japanese species, *M. sieboldii* is also reported to occur in discrete populations in ten Chinese provinces, and so far as I know morphological differences have not been reported elsewhere.

There are further distinguishing characters in addition to those specified by Dr Spongberg. The flowers of *M. sinensis* are distinct from *M. sieboldii*: pendent rather than nodding, with nine rather than typically six tepals, notably saucer shaped rather than cup shaped and at maturity much larger and flatter in profile. The leaf veins number 10–15 rather than 7–9, and the floral internodes (conspicuous zones extending from a scar on the peduncle left by a spathaceous bract up to the base of the flower) are significantly longer.

I hold that these distinguishing features in total are significant and substantial: sufficient to separate the two as distinct species.

The *Magnolia wilsonii* alliance

All species within the Oyama section are closely allied to the point where *The Flora of China* places them in a new genus of *Oyama*, (recognising *Oyama sinensis* at species level). There is certainly a case for regarding *M. sinensis* as more closely allied to *M. wilsonii*, with floral characters, stipule scars, peduncle and pale pink fruit aggregates sufficiently close to consider it as a subspecies.

Indeed, it is not unlikely that a majority of plants in UK gardens labelled *M. sinensis* are hybrids of *M. wilsonii*. The entire history of *M. sinensis* is one of misidentification (both *M. wilsonii* and *M. sinensis* were at one time labelled as the long-since-sunk *M. nicholsoniana*), lost labels, an absence of records and a wide distribution of open-pollinated seed over many years. As Lord Aberconway remarked at the RHS Tree and Shrub conference in 1938: "Plants of *M. wilsonii* and *M. sinensis* are growing quite close together at Lanarth and have seeded

Magnolia sinensis **showing distinctive leaf, bud and shoot** – *photo:* **Tom Hudson**

freely there. The generous distribution of seed gathered from *M. sinensis* has led to the growing of a number of plants which have proved to be hybrids between the two species."

The classic example is *M. × highdownensis*, originally thought to be a hybrid and now generally regarded as a form of *M. wilsonii*.

The superb clone now widely grown internationally as *M. sinensis* is probably the form propagated vegetatively and previously available from a few commercial outlets as *M. sinensis* 'Grandiflora', which of course could be of hybrid origin.

Be that as it may, there are material differences between *M. sinensis* and the type of *M. wilsonii*. First, the leaf blades of the former are readily distinguished as larger, broadly obovate to suborbicular, rounded with an occasional mucronate tip, dark green and stiff and chartaceous at maturity. There are usually villous crinkled hairs on the lower surface, though this character is said to be variable. I have seen a recent reintroduction of *M. sinensis* from seed collected by Mikinori Ogisu in western Sichuan, which although still juvenile and thus too early to take a defining view, shows clear elements of these leaf characters.

By contrast, *M. wilsonii* typically has elliptic to narrowly ovate, pointed leaves with the widest point normally below halfway. They have a brownish pubescence when young, turning yellowish or greyish-white when mature. According to Johnstone "no plants with obovate rounded leaves have yet been raised from typical *M. wilsoni*", an observation I can readily endorse. Johnstone also records that plants raised from seed from typical *M. sinensis* at Caerhays and elsewhere exhibited the distinctive foliage and shoot characters of the parent.

Second, there is a notable and consistent difference in the twigs, with *M. sinensis* having a light fawn bark in contrast with the dark purplish brown of *M. wilsonii*.

Third, an echo of Wilson's description of a "straggling shrub" lies in the habit of *M. sinensis* in cultivation – a multistemmed shrub wider than high. Johnstone describes the big plant at Caerhays in 1945 as 16ft high by 34ft wide – width more than double the height. Its flowering is spread over a considerable period.

M. wilsonii is by comparison normally a quite neat, contained, rather upright shrub or small tree (thus generally suitable for a small garden). It usually flowers freely in a main burst, with but few flowers to follow the initial impressive display.

The *Magnolia globosa* connection

It is not entirely surprising that the original Wilson introduction was designated *M. globosa* ssp. *sinensis*, a new variant of *M. globosa*. The foliage is similar. The leaf blades of typical *M. globosa* are near to *M. sinensis* – large, up to 25cm long, usually obovate, elliptic or broadly ovate, dark green, the reverse with crinkled, usually rufous hairs. The stipule scars extend more than half the length of the petiole. It also has a wide spreading habit.

However, the flowers of *M. globosa* have a singular, individual quality – usually nodding, narrowly cup shaped or egg shaped (the Nepalese vernacular term for the species is the 'hen' magnolia) up to about 6cm across and sometimes stained or marked with pink or purple. These contrast with the large, pendent saucers up to 12cm across of *M. sinensis*. The fruit aggregates are notably smaller, and crimson rather than pale pink.

Four forms and hybrids of **M. wilsonii** – the foliage bottom right shows **M. globosa** influence

Flowers of **M. wilsonii** (left), **M. sieboldii** (centre) and **M. globosa** (right) **for comparison** – *photos:* **Maurice Foster**

***Magnolia sinensis* at the Savill Garden, Windsor**

***M. sinensis* reverse of leaf** – *photos:* **John Anderson**

Conclusion

The distinguishing characters between *M. sinensis* and *M. sieboldii* are consistent and substantial and certainly sufficient to regard the two taxa as separate and distinct entities. Most authorities and authors over many years since Stapf, such as Bean and Johnstone, maintained *M. sinensis* as a species. Even authors publishing after the 1976 Spongberg revision, such as Treseder and Callaway, among others, have chosen nonetheless to continue to maintain it as a species.

The alliance with *M. wilsonii*, while close, does not warrant going so far as to treat it as a subspecies or even as within the range of variation of that species, which is considerable. The striking, consistent, and reproducible differences in foliage, shoot and habit preclude this conclusion.

Online, there is widespread division – The RHS, the Rhododendron, Camellia & Magnolia Group and some nurseries follow the Spongberg subspecies revision, while many others, such as the authoritative International Dendrology Society Trees and Shrubs Online, continue to maintain it as a species.

This unresolved question needs resolution; the status of *M. sinensis* needs clarifying; and the evidence plainly indicates that the safest conclusion is to maintain it at species level.

REFERENCES

Hunt, David (ed), *Magnolias and their allies,* published for the IDS and the Magnolia Society
Treseder, Neil G, *Magnolias,* Faber
The Flora of China – online
Sargent, CS (ed), *Plantae Wilsonianae,* Diosorides Press
Callaway, Dorothy J, *The World of Magnolias,* Timber Press
Johnstone, G H, *Asiatic Magnolias in Cultivation,* RHS Ornamental Flowering Trees and Shrubs conference report 38, RHS

Maurice Foster vmh *is an Honorary Member of the Woody Plant Committee, a Trustee of the Tree Register of Britain and Ireland and a former Chairman of the Group.*

A few more alpine rhododendrons

Barry Starling

John Good's article in last year's Yearbook brought deserved recognition to a colourful group of plants for the smaller garden, though they are equally suitable for larger gardens too. Here follows an account of yet more small rhododendrons of varying characteristics, but all worthwhile additions to any collection.

About 55 years ago I imported from Hakoneya Nurseries, Tokyo, ten plants of *Rhododendron aureum*, one of which I supplied to a keen plantswoman who had lived in Japan and was making herself feel at home by surrounding herself with Japanese native plants. A few months later she telephoned me to say how pleased she was that her little shrub had flowered with corollas of soft yellow with a striking red flare in the throat. *R. aureum* of course, is normally plain yellow, which is how the remaining plants flowered in due course. Sadly the recipient of the red-flared variety died shortly afterwards and her husband dispersed her collection as a priority! I've never located that particular variant since.

• *R. aureum* is a mainly prostrate, woody little shrub flowering early in the year with small trusses of up to eight flowers ranging from pale to lemon yellow; each corolla is up to 3cm long. Coming from north Japan northwards to the Altai mountains in Russia it is extremely hardy and although very slow growing presents no problems in cultivation. In Russia, plant hunter Konstantin Cherezov writes of *R. aureum*: "It is unusual to find rhododendrons in a clay, dense substrate of residual hard rocks. Of course there is nothing here that could be called peat. *R. aureum* is very compact in such conditions on Serpentine soils on the border of Khakassia and Tuva mountain tundra".

Rhododendron aureum
– all photos: **Barry Starling**

Some 300 years ago a tincture of *R. aureum* leaves was used as a cure for arthritis but it was reluctantly abandoned when it had to be admitted that it killed more people than it cured! I cannot help wondering if in the light of modern scientific practice it might be worth researchers taking another look at it.

• *R. glaucophyllum* ssp. *glaucophyllum* can reach 1.5m in height but is normally to be found in gardens at barely 1m high. Readily identified by the very glaucous undersides of the 3–5cm oblong-lanceolate leaves, it produces an abundance of rosy-pink bells in lax, four to eight-flowered trusses. Long established in cultivation as a reliable species from around or above the snow line in the Himalayas, it is hardy throughout the UK.

A white-flowered form was collected as seed in Nepal, in 1971 by Beer, Lancaster and Morris. Among those receiving a share of the seed was Kath Dryden from Essex, who raised a good crop of seedlings among which was

Rhododendron glaucophyllum 'Len Beer'

R. hanceanum 'Nanum'

one outstanding in the quality and size of its pure white flowers. In 1977 this was exhibited before the RHS awards committee where it received an Award of Merit subject to naming. When news came through of the untimely death of intrepid plant hunter Len Beer, a member of the expedition responsible for introducing this plant, Kath Dryden thought it fitting that it should be named in his honour.

Kath passed her plant on to me with instructions to propagate and circulate it. One of those requesting a plant was Len's 90-year-old mother, a request I was pleased to fulfil. When I delivered this plant to her in Devon, I was confronted by a superb display of pot geraniums, fuchsias and a whole host of other colourful specimens. It was easy to see from whom Len had inherited his love of plants!

A geographical variant of *R. glaucophyllum* from further east in the Himalayan chain, *R. glaucophyllum* ssp. *tubiforme* only differs from the type in its longer corolla tube and slightly larger, more open habit.

• **R. hanceanum** The type form of *R. hanceanum* is rarely seen in gardens, the cultivar 'Canton Consul' usually being planted. This has small, cream trusses on a neat very compact shrub of about 60cm in height, 1m in diameter. Well clothed with leaves it flowers reliably freely in April–May. Less often encountered is a smaller, more

compact version with truly yellow flowers, *R. hanceanum* 'Nanum' a choice little shrub that is not always easy to please though well worth the effort. It is most compact in a position of full light where it will respond with a multitude of flowers.

First discovered in 1886 on Mount Omei, Szechuan, the species was subsequently introduced by Wilson in its dwarfer form under the number W 4255.

• **R. kongboense** Though having grown *R. kongboense* for many years I had no idea that the species existed with flowers of any colour other than red. These can be from palest pink through deeper, rose pink but the red-flowered one is perhaps most worthy of a place in the garden. With typical Pogonanthum type flowers, small, tubular and

R. kongboense

borne a little more sparsely than others in the section, the shrub has a more or less fastigiate habit, which may be less attractive than other close relatives such as *R. primuliflorum* or *R. cephalanthum* but its intense rosy-red colouring can be quite endearing.

Kingdon Ward certainly liked it. In *A Plant Hunter in Tibet* he writes "At an altitude of 13,000ft. I found deep snow but also beautiful dwarf rhododendrons in bloom: the crouching *R. sanguineum*, incandescent with blood red flowers, and aromatic blooms of *R. kongboense*, its coral red flowers clustered into orbs which shook in the wind".

R. kongboense was first discovered in the Kongbo Valley of south east Tibet by Kingdon Ward who comments on the use of the shrub in high class religious ceremonies to burn as incense, its foliage being very fragrant.

A cultivar introduced by Ness Botanic Garden as *R. kongboense* 'Redness', deep rosy-red in colour and robust in habit with deep-green leaved stems well clustered with large inflorescences, is one to look out for.

• ***R. luteiflorum*** is undoubtedly one of my favourites, especially the collection KW 21556 to be found under the cultivar name 'Glencoy'. Even Davidian, who usually confines himself to strict botanical detail, in his book *The Rhododendron Species* enthuses with "It is one of the finest yellow flowered dwarf rhododendrons in cultivation".

During many years in my cold Essex garden including the notorious 1962/63 winter it came through unharmed and for 36 years has withstood Dartmoor's wildest weather with equanimity. The flowers, which come in March–April and often again in late autumn, even December, can be damaged by frost but remarkably, usually escape. *R. luteiflorum* makes a shrub roughly 1m by 1m with elliptic leaves of up to 8cm in length, glaucous beneath and borne on stems with attractive peeling, chestnut-brown bark. Clear yellow, campanulate corollas are three to six per truss, though mostly nearer six than three. Flowers of 'Glencoy' are bigger and of more substance than type.

R. luteiflorum was found by Kingdon Ward in north Myanmar (Upper Burma) between the River Nmai and the Mali Hka, branches of the Irrawaddy. It was introduced as recently as 1953, being first thought to be a variety of *R. glaucophyllum*.

R. luteiflorum 'Glencoy' received an RHS First Class Certificate in 1966 for a plant shown by Brodick Castle Gardens on the Isle of Arran.

• ***R. mucronulatum*** in its type form resembles a larger version of *R. dauricum*, flowering any time from December to March. While flower colour varies from pale pink to deep rose purple or white, one of the best being the cultivar 'Cornell Pink' and even better a

Rhododendron luteiflorum 'Glencoy'

R. mucronulatum 'Cheju Dwarf' or var. taquetii

R. pemakoense

R. russatum **Dark Form**

hybrid between that and 'Woodland Pink'. These, however, make shrubs of up to 2m in height but one that fits more neatly into the subject of this article is a dwarf plant from the island of Cheju off the southern tip of South Korea. Not exceeding about 45cm it is compact and bushy producing its abundant purple-red flowers in late February–March. These will stand a few degrees of frost but the buds are hardier so that the loss of an initial display may be replaced by a further one.

First introduced as *R. mucronulatum* var. *chejuense* it was then described by Davidian as *R. mucronulatum* var. *taquetii*. It is mainly deciduous but not always completely so and hardy, though flowering as it does in winter the flowers will not withstand the frosts of colder parts of the UK.

• *R. pemakoense* was collected blind by Kingdon Ward in 1924. That is, he collected seed at the end of November on cliffs overlooking the Tsangpo Gorge, by burrowing down through the snow where he discovered the dwarf species just a few inches high and loaded with flower buds.

In cultivation *R. pemakoense* retains its dwarf habit, slowly increasing its diameter over the years, spreading by underground runners to the extent that one in my garden at 40 years old, though only 60cm high is 3m long by 2m across. It tends to make a flat-topped shrub on which a blanket of snow may

settle, even during the flowering season but I have had this thaw leaving the flowers undamaged. Light pink flowers are produced in such abundance as to largely hide the foliage each being widely funnel shaped and up to 5cm in diameter. Incidentally a cross between the species and *R. keiskei* var. *ozawae* 'Yaku Fairy' has yielded *R.* 'Pemako Fairy', an even dwarfer plant with blush-pink flowers that are so crowded as to be obscene, when grown in full light. However, in shade a more respectable crop of flowers will be produced, each attractively backed by green leaves.

On older plants the habit of progressively spreading into new soil can lead to the centre becoming starved so that it is a good idea to work into the crown leaf mould or well-rotted cow manure from time to time.

Ledum 'Teshio' x *R. russatum*

• *R. russatum* from western China varies in the wild considerably in size, habit and the intensity of its flower colour but the

Rhododendron saluenense KW6991

R. lepidotum var. elaeagnoides

best garden plants tend to be compact, well foliaged, no more than 60cm high and with corollas of a deep rich purple. Predominant among these are the Award of Merit form shown by A.M. Williams in 1927 and described as intense violet-blue, and the deep purple one that received a First Class Certificate in 1933 when exhibited by Lionel de Rothschild, Exbury. In 1938 *R. russatum* received a very well-deserved Award of Garden Merit.

The species flowers freely in mid-April with trusses of up to six, 2cm wide corollas, which are reasonably hardy. Dark green, broadly elliptic to oblong or oval leaves are dark brown beneath due to a dense covering of scales. Found in the wild at 3,500–4,500m in north Yunnan, into Szechuan on rocky hillsides or alpine meadows often with other moorland rhododendron species or other small shrubs such as cassiope, berberis or potentilla, and interspersed with *Lilium lophophorum* and *Fritillaria delavayii* seeking its protection from grazing animals.

R. russatum has been used as the pollen parent to create hybrids with *R. groenlandicum* (formerly *Ledum*) both in Sweden and the UK. That the cross is possible is of interest but the resultant hybrids, with their inferior palest blue to white flowers and a gawky habit are not garden worthy.

• *R. saluenense* ssp. *saluenense* has been a favourite of mine for many years in its dwarfer form. Its almost prostrate habit, deep claret, 2cm wide flowers set it apart from others of its ilk. Tending to flower spasmodically, it is at its most showy in April/May but can produce a flower or two during the autumn. By this time the leaves will have turned chocolate-red.

Its wide range over the eastern end of the Himalayas to the Salween River into Yunnan includes forms with flowers of varying shades of rose and growing from 15cm up to 1m tall, of lax habit but that most commonly seen in cultivation is the smaller, more compact one. There is a white flowered, prostrate form on the Beima-shan but I am not sure if this has found its way into cultivation yet.

R. saluenense ssp. *chameunum* covers many acres of mountainside in China, Myanmar and Tibet where plants can be 1m high but are usually 50cm or less and flower colour varies from wishy-washy pink to a good, deep rose or purple-rose. One form collected by Forrest in 1914 (F 12968) has 3cm diameter corollas, deep rose spotted red on the upper lobes.

• *R. lepidotum* On the alpine meadows of west Sikkim, above 3,500m, three small species predominate – *R. anthopogon*, *lepidotum* and *setosum*, all growing in virtually identical habitat. Why is it then that when brought into cultivation one is perfectly easy to grow, one grows well enough but is very shy to flower, and one is very difficult to please?

R. setosum 'Crimson'

R. setosum in the landscape

R. lepidotum, a deciduous species, is the easy one, flowering in May with usually purple but sometimes pink, purple-rose or rarely white corollas while its smaller, higher altitude variety *R. lepidotum* var. *elaeagnoides* has yellow flowers. *R. anthopogon*, too, is no problem to grow but steadfastly refuses to flower for me except in the cultivar 'Betty Graham' introduced by the Cox's of Glendoick, and which received an Award of Merit in 1969.

    This reluctance to flower of plants from the Sikkim collection of seed (1983 Alpine Garden Society expedition) is so disappointing as it is there the western Himalayan form of *R. anthopogon*, namely *R. hypenanthum*, meets one from the eastern end to produce plants with pink, apricot, pale orange and salmon inflorescences over sometimes silver-grey foliage.

R. shweliense

of many of the plants in cultivation under that name. My plant I have had for over 45 years and it ticks all the boxes. It does not have features of the alternatives suggested so I am assuming it is the genuine article.

    R. shweliense was introduced in 1924 by George Forrest (24154) from the Shweli-Salween Divide, west Yunnan where it grows on cliffs and rocky areas at 3,000–3,350m. In cultivation it has proved perfectly hardy, flowering towards the end of May with bell-shaped corollas, 1.5cm across, which are an unusual shade of honey-yellow flushed rose. Narrowly elliptic leaves up to 4cm long tend to be slightly glaucous beneath, clothing a moderately compact shrub attaining a height of about 60cm. An open situation seems to suit the species which deserves to be more widely grown.

• **R. setosum** The third species, *R. setosum*, in the wild can be spectacular with the intensity of colour from prodigiously produced flowers of deep purple, carmine or pink. I believe the species is happier in Scotland where colder winters give it an enforced rest. In the wild, *R. setosum* makes cushions of compact growth 30cm high and up to 1m in diameter flowering in late May/June. With me, however, it sulked for many years with hardly a bloom produced.

• **R. shweliense** Of *R. shweliense*, some leading botanists have cast doubt on the authenticity

• *R. trichostomum* With an inflorescence described as a racemose-umbel *R. trichostomum* is often likened to plants of the genus daphne. Individual flowers consist of a slender tube up to 8mm in length with flaring corolla lobes to a diameter of 1cm. Of the several different varieties and cultivars, some have received RHS awards, and I have grown three of these, all of which I would recommend. First is *R. trichostomum* var. *ledoides*, which reaches about 60cm tall, covering itself with white flowers in May/June; the second is 'Rae Berry' from western USA, with larger white flowers. Rae Berry helped set up the American Rhododendron Species Foundation and put together a very impressive collection of rhododendrons of her own; the third is *R. trichostomum* var. *ledoides* 'Collingwood Ingram' with noteworthy rose-pink flowers that earned it a First Class Certificate from the RHS in 1976. Others to look out for are a form of *R. trichostomum* var. *ledoides* called 'Quarry Wood' with inflorescences flushed red-purple (A.M. 1971) and similarly coloured *R. trichostomum* var. *radinum* 'Sweet Bay' (A.M. 1960 and AGM 1993).

Another excellent species from western China, that home of so many good alpine rhododendrons, it grows on mountain slopes above the tree line or extends down into thin woodland. In the garden an open situation in plenty of light will keep the shrub compact.

Even among the dwarf species of the genus rhododendron, plants can be so diverse as to find a suitable niche in almost every garden. Having relatively small root balls, the abhorrence of many (but not all) to lime can be catered for while their often-windswept homelands make them tolerant of increasing gales in our changing climate. Flowers of almost every hue are produced in plenty while their different flowering seasons ensure colour for the first six months of the year. Few alpine species have fragrant flowers but several, especially the Pogonanthums, have spicily scented foliage. Truly these are worthwhile additions to any garden.

R. trichostomum var. *ledoides* 'Collingwood Ingram'

R. trichostomum var. *ledoides* 'Rae Berry'

R. trichostomum var. *radinum*

Barry Starling AOH *was a keen grower and hybridiser of Ericaceae from his teens and enjoyed studying many of them in the wild.*

A Prussian princess or a virgin from Lombardy?
The entangled history of *Camellia japonica* cultivars 'Vergine di Collebeato' and 'Princesse de Prusse'

Brigitte Wachsmuth

Camellia 'Vergine di Collebeato' – *photo:* **Dr Gianmario Motta**

For many decades Camellia 'Vergine di Collebeato' was thought to be lost and only known from images, as was the variety 'Princesse de Prusse'. In this text, the events that took place in connection with their introduction in 1856/57 are described and evidence is provided that they are the same cultivar. The confusion and inaccuracies surrounding the introduction of 'Vergine di Collebeato' will be clarified. The German nurseryman Alfred Topf, notorious for renaming cultivars of Italian origin, is identified as the originator of the re-naming as 'Prinzessin von

**Camellia 'Vergine di Collebeato' exhibiting
another pattern** – *photo:* **Dr Gianmario Motta**

---

*Preussen', which subsequently was translated by
Ambroise Verschaffelt as 'Princesse de Prusse'.*

The crème de la crème of camellias is made
up of the 'formal doubles', which are
varieties with 'many rows of regular, imbricate
petals and no stamens', according to the
definition given by the International Camellia
Society. The varieties with spirally arranged
petals occupy a special position among formal
doubles. There are not too many of them and
one of the modern, better-known varieties is
'Sawada's Dream' [1959 USA], although the
spiral arrangement of its formal double flower
is rare. The unusual spiral arrangement among
formal double-flowering camellia has occurred
repeatedly since the introduction of camellias
into western gardens, but only with some of
them is it so stable that it affects the majority
of the flowers. The luxurious perfection of the
clearly set-off rows of petals curved in a gentle
arc from the centre to the periphery
enchanted the Victorian public.

As earlier *Camellia japonica* varieties named
'Spiralis' (France 1830 introduction) and
'Spiraliter Imbricata' (Italy 1840) suggest,
this type of flower form was not completely
unknown in 1857. Even so the description
of the variety 'Virgine di Collebeato'
accompanied by a plate in Louis van Houtte's
Flore des Serres of 1857 was received with
disbelief by many. The image depicting a
flower with seven very regularly arranged
concentric spiral arms seemed to be an
idealised representation and this was not
uncommon in illustrated garden magazines at
that time. But as we know now, it was accurate.

The variety is spelt 'Vergine di Collebeato'
today. According to the International Camellia
Register, it was listed for the first time in the
1846 catalogue of the Ghent gardener
Alexandre Verschaffelt, but without a
description. Upon investigation this
information does not stand up. A camellia
under this name or a similar one is not listed
in any of the Verschaffelt catalogues (1844–
1869) kept in the catalogue collection at
Wageningen University in the Netherlands.
There is another reason why it is most unlikely
that the Établissement Verschaffelt could have
held the variety by 1846. When Ambroise
Verschaffelt included it in the *Nouvelle
Iconographie des Caméllias* in 1858 as 'Virgine
Calubini' he mentioned that he had received it
from Italy only the year before. Italian sources
give "about 1850" as the date
of origin, such as in the well-known *Antiche
Camelie del Lago Maggiore* by Piero Hillebrand
and Gianbattista Bertolazzi of 2003. With
certainty it was exhibited by Cesare
Franchetti, a well-known camellia enthusiast
from Florence, as 'Vergine Colubini' in 1856 at
the Third Exposition of the Tuscan
Horticultural Society.

Van Houtte gives a certain Pietro Torre as
the presumed breeder but a man of this name
has not been identified and a 'Pietro' Torre
may not have existed at all. The variety was

Camellia 'Vergine di Collebeato' from Van Houtte's journal *Flore des Serres*, July 1857

Camellia 'Princesse de Prusse' from Verschaffelt's *Nouvelle Iconographie des Caméllias* 8th issue, August 1857

also offered to Van Houtte under the name 'Vergine Calubini'. However Van Houtte preferred the name 'Virgine di Collebeato'. Collebeato near Brescia was the home of Conte Giuseppe Torre. The garden of his villa has now become what is called locally 'Parco 1°Maggio'. In 1857 Conte Guiseppe travelled to Milan to exhibit 'Vergine di Collebeato' as a novelty. In Collebeato there is a small shrine dedicated to the Virgin Mary, who is said to have appeared there between 1700 and 1750. She is venerated as the 'Virgin of Calvarola' or 'Virgin of Collebeato', which confirms this town as the place of origin.

The different name of 'Vergine Colubini' or 'Vergine Calubini' is puzzling. It may be a person's name but it seems more likely that it is a corruption of 'Collebeato' as there are three corresponding consonants. 'Colubini', which is the earliest form, has its first three letters in common with 'Collebeato'. In a time when plant labels were largely handwritten,

Camellia 'Virgine Calubini' – from Verschaffelt's *Nouvelle Iconographie des Caméllias* 11th issue, November 1858

handwriting could easily be misread; so this is the likeliest explanation and Franchetti, who lived miles away in Florence, seems to be the source of this mistake.

Leaving aside the spelling variants, the fact remains that the variety was circulating under two different names by 1857. As by this date another actor had already appeared on the scene, the German nurseryman Alfred Topf. In May 1856, Topf had bought up the entire stock of 'Vergine di Collebeato' from "a certain Torre", believing that he had the right to rename it and to be the exclusive distributor. In the *Generalanzeiger*, a trade journal of which he was the editor, he later wrote that he felt entitled to "give the variety a more fitting name". It is not completely certain whether the seller was Giuseppe Torre or the otherwise unknown Pietro Torre. What is known is that Conte Giuseppe Torre still owned at least one specimen, which he exhibited in Milan in 1857, the following year. Topf offered the cultivar, renamed as 'Prinzessin von Preussen', by subscription throughout Europe, in 1856. Then in 1857, Ambroise Verschaffelt portrayed the variety as 'Princesse de Prusse' in his *Nouvelle Iconographie*, but before the name 'Virgine Calubini' appeared. Obviously Verschaffelt did not realise that two names existed for the same camellia.

Alfred Topf (1820–1897) was the owner of a nursery in Erfurt, at that time a centre of horticulture in Germany. As a young man, Topf travelled to England, France and Belgium. He worked for major nurseries like Jean-Baptiste Ryfkogel in Paris, Simon-Louis Frères in Metz and, as a travelling agent, for Louis van Houtte in Ghent. About 1845 he founded his own nursery in Erfurt. Topf was a busy and energetic man who published popular booklets and articles in garden journals aspiring to rival Louis van Houtte's firm as the leading European nursery. In 1847 he leased the Erfurt Botanical Garden from the Prussian government. The Botanical Garden had got into difficulties due to political changes in the years after the

Napoleonic wars. Instead of a payment, Topf committed himself to establish and maintain a gardeners' training college in its grounds. In 1853, he was elected president of the Erfurt Horticultural Society. Unfortunately, the nursery had to declare bankruptcy in 1856. Topf however acted as editor of the *Generalanzeiger Journal* from 1857–1859 until the college was closed and he was arrested and imprisoned for not paying off his debts. Despite some attempts Topf never managed to set up a gardening business again after his release from prison. 'Vergine di Collebeato' was not the first acquisition by Topf that he had renamed. In 1850 he had acquired the original mother plant of an Italian magnolia called 'Mahomet' with its grafted progeny. The magnolia became world-famous as *M.* 'Lennei', the name given it by Topf (see 2016 Yearbook article by Brigitte Wachsmuth).

Topf had announced his acquisition as 'Prinzessin von Preussen' in 1856, but he did not release the plants to the subscribers until 1858. Messrs. Moschkowitz & Siegling, another nursery located in Erfurt, was already able to offer the variety by October 1857 at an even lower price than Topf in his subscription offer. Verschaffelt states that Topf had conveyed part of his stock to F.A. Haage, one of the largest nurseries in Erfurt, and another batch was purchased by Verschaffelt himself. It is possible that these deliveries had already taken place in 1857 with Moschkowitz & Siegling among these privileged customers. This is the most likely presumption. It is rather unlikely that Moschkowitz & Siegling had imported the cultivar from Italy adopting the name 'Prinzessin von Preussen' because it was already widely known from Topf's announcement.

Verschaffelt offered the plant as 'Princesse de Prusse', which the International Camellia Register records as a valid name. 'Princess of Prussia' is accepted as its synonym, despite the fact that in 1860 Milne & Co, a British nursery in Vauxhall, London exhibited a 'Princess of Prussia' camellia described as being "pure white streaked with pink". 'Virgine Calubini' is considered as an "erroneously given" synonym by the Register. However, the Register does not at present recognise the original German form of the name, 'Prinzessin von Preussen'.

Topf's renaming did not go unnoticed. The editors of leading German gardening journals made what are, more or less, derogatory comments. But Topf saw only himself as being in the right, even more so when he found out that a specimen of 'Vergine Calubini', which he had bought for a large amount turned out to be the same variety. He vented his anger in his characteristically pompous and verbose style and with thoroughly nationalistic undertones towards the "Belgian gentlemen, the accountants of European floristry" who he thought might suppress the name 'Prinzessin von Preussen' thereby ignoring his rights. What his rights should have been in this situation is just as difficult to understand as is Topf's conviction expressed a few lines later, that the name he had provided, had "priority". In addition, his accusation was quite unfair as the Belgian Verschaffelt had already made a permanent record of 'Princesse de Prusse' and given Topf credit for the introduction, in the *Nouvelle Iconographie*.

The question of priority however needs to be discussed further. The variety was exhibited as 'Vergine Colubini' in 1856 in Florence without a description and probably with a corrupted name. Topf had announced the subscription in the garden journal *Deutsches Magazin für Garten-und Blumenkunde* as early as September 1856 accompanied by a brief description. Its anonymous author signed it as "O.R.". In February 1857, a detailed description and a coloured plate followed in the same publication. O.R. therefore gave the first valid description of the cultivar. The plate has to be regarded as the first representation, because Van Houtte's description and plate were published some months later. With almost absolute certainty Giuseppe Torre is the breeder whereas

Camellia 'Princesse de Prusse' – the first illustration of the cultivar in the February issue of the journal *Deutsches Magazin für Garten-und Blumenkunde* 1857

"Pietro" Torre may be just a mistake on the part of Louis van Houtte. Using the name 'Vergine di Collebeato' at the 1857 exhibition in Milan, Torre indicated that he still insisted on the original name. Topf himself conceded the renaming and stated that plants named 'Vergine Calubini' – a valid synonym of 'Vergine di Collebeato' – are the same cultivar. 'Prinzessin von Preussen' therefore has to be regarded as a synonym of the latter, and 'Princesse de Prusse' as a synonymous translation. Finally 1856 has to be regarded as the correct year of introduction.

Die Gartenwelt 1931 (the last vestige) –
the flower at the bottom right is
Camellia 'Prinzessin von Preussen'

In the 20th century, the cultivar was still known as 'Prinzessin von Preussen' in Germany. In 1931 it was depicted on a coloured pull-out in the journal *Die Gartenwelt* along with other varieties and recommended as an extraordinary cultivar. But all traces of the name and cultivar 'Prinzessin von Preussen' or 'Princesse de Prusse' have subsequently disappeared. *Camellia* 'Vergine di Collebeato' was long thought to be lost: but it was rediscovered in 1964 in a garden near Lake Maggiore. Other localities with old specimens have come to light since: for example at the Botanical Institute in Batumi, a Black Sea resort in Georgia, where the variety was included in a collection of 19th century camellias. 'Vergine di Collebeato' is also now found in France, Germany and Australia, but it is as the emblem of the Italian Camellia Society that it has really received renown, making it an outstanding symbol of the Italian passion for this unique cultivar.
In the book published by Regione Piemonte

Camelie dell' Ottocento nel Verbano (2003) Dr Andrea Corneo remarks about this camellia that "The flowers do not always show the special characteristics. The percentage of spiral flowers and the perfection of the latter essentially depend on the environmental and meteorological conditions." The remarkable seven spiralled form of 'Vergine di Collebeato' may not be frequently seen, but once seen, it can never be forgotten.

REFERENCES

[anon.] (1857) *Deutsches Magazin für Garten- und Blumenkunde* p33 plus plate
[anon.] (1857) *L'Esposizione dei fiori in Milano nel marzo del 1857. Il giardiniere: Annali d'orticultura* 4,9 (6) p100
Giel, F. (1931) Vergesst nicht die Kamelien! *Die Gartenwelt*, issue 14/1931 p189 plus pull-out
The International Camellia Register records for 'Vergine di Collebeato' and 'Princesse de Prusse'
O. R. (1856) *Camellia* Prinzessin von Preussen, *Deutsches Magazin für Garten- und Blumenkunde* 1856, issue 12 pp366/367
Società toscana di orticoltura (1856) Catalogo degli oggetti presentati alla terza esposizione fatta in Firenze p8
Topf, Alfred (1859) Eine Probe aus dem Handelsverkehr, *General-Anzeiger für Kunst- und Handelsgärtnerei*, 1859/9 front page
van Houtte, Louis (1857) *Flore des Serres* vol. 12 p.125, plate 1245
Verschaffelt, Ambroise (1857) *Nouvelle Iconographie des Caméllias* issue 8 plate 2
Verschaffelt, Ambroise (1858) *Nouvelle Iconographie des Caméllias* issue 11 plate 2
Wachsmuth, Brigitte (2016) A minor mistake from 1916: *RHS Rhododendrons, Camellias & Magnolias Yearbook* 2016 pp211–214
Corneo, Andrea; Remotti, Dora (2003) *Camelie dell' Ottocento nel Verbano*. Torino : Regione Piemonte p236
Hillebrand, Piero; Bertolazzi, Gianbattista (2003) *Antiche Camelie del Lago Maggiore*. Verbania-Intra: Alberti Libraio Editore p361

Brigitte Wachsmuth *is an author and garden historian from Bielefeld, Germany, focusing on ornamental plants.*

The amazing variety of the newest magnolia hybrids

Charles Williams

The publication of Beat Heerdegen and Reto Eisenhut's splendid book on *Magnoliaceae* in late 2019 demonstrates all too clearly how magnolia hybridisation and breeding has moved on apace in the past 20 years. The text may be in German but the photographs and breeding records are not. There are many pages devoted to 'crosses and new things'.

Hopefully, it will be of interest to Rhododendron, Camellia & Magnolia Group members for us to try to share our experience and views on some of the best results we have seen in the expanding National Plant Collection of *Magnolia* here at Caerhays. The varieties selected here for special mention are only a few of the 80 or so that have been photographed in flower here for the first time over the past few years in The Garden Diary (thediary.caerhays.co.uk).

These new varieties represent the work of a number of magnolia breeders from all around the world but, in particular, by Philippe de Spoelberch at the Arboretum Wespelaar in Belgium, Vance Hooper, Ian Baldick and Peter Cave in New Zealand, Otto and Reto Eisenhut in Switzerland and Michael Gottschalk in Germany. In the UK, Maurice Foster, John Carlson and the late John Gallagher have created and introduced exciting new hybrids.

To try to introduce newer varieties for consideration, this article deliberately ignores all 14 of the now better-known varieties selected by Jim Gardiner, John Gallagher and myself for the article on Up-and-coming 'new' magnolias published in the 2016 yearbook. Varieties bred and raised at Caerhays and registered with Magnolia Society International in recent years, are also deliberately ignored here because they have also featured in Rhododendron, Camellia & Magnolia Group yearbooks and been seen at both RHS and Cornwall Garden Society spring shows.

Like any assessment of this sort one can only apologise for personal preferences. The performance of some New Zealand hybrids in our UK climate has not corresponded to the colouration of the flowers or the growth rates of the young trees in their home environment. Magnolia hybrids can, and do, perform differently in wet and warmer Cornish conditions from those of the continent with harsher winters. Varieties that do well in the Valley Gardens at Windsor, with annual rainfall half that in Cornwall, can grow less well here and vice versa. Air temperatures can clearly influence the flower colouration of individual magnolias from year to year.

There is, however, no doubt that these new hybrids allow all magnolia growers to choose and enjoy something genuinely new and different in terms of flower colours, plant size and the timing of flowering.

One element of confusion to recognise at the outset is that several of the best new crosses have been made available for sale in the nursery trade initially as unnamed hybrid crosses between two named parents or disguised for patenting purposes. Then, at a later date, individual names have been allocated and registered to the same plants. In this article I have used the subsequent registered name while giving details of the parentage involved.

43

Hybrids using Caerhays-bred magnolias as one parent

All photos: **Caerhays Estate**

• *M.* 'Anne Leitner'
(*M.* 'Black Tulip' x *M.* 'J C Williams')
One of Michael Gottschalk's best new introductions from 2014, this was planted here in 2016 and first flowered only three years later. It has large wine-red flowers and looks to be developing into a large tree.

• *M.* 'A E Bold'
(*M.* 'Black Tulip' x *M.* 'J C Williams')
This was hybridised by Michael Gottschalk and registered only in 2018. The Caerhays plant was planted in 2015 (without its subsequent name) and has developed into a tree with a narrow upright habit and large cup-shaped Bordeaux-red flowers. It has flowered copiously for the past couple of years and is smaller growing than 'Anne Leitner' with a slender crown.

• *M.* 'Black Swan' (*M.* 'Pickard's Ruby' x *M.* 'Caerhays Surprise')
John Carlson raised this exceptional cross in Gwent, Wales, which was registered in 2007. It has dark red-purple flowers and, as you would expect from both its parents, it has a smaller growing shrubby habit rather than becoming a tree. It has yet to produce more than a couple of flowers here, but I doubt we will have to wait long.

• *M.* 'Blushing Belle'
(*M.* 'Yellow Bird' x *M.* 'Caerhays Belle')
A US cross between *M.* 'Yellow Bird' and *M.* 'Caerhays Belle', the flowers of *M.* 'Blushing Belle' have more than a trace of yellow as they open.

Outstanding new hybrids involving *Magnolia* 'Black Tulip'

It should be no surprise that this popular and increasingly well-known variety has been used as the parent for some exceptional new hybrids.

• *M.* 'Aphrodite'
(*M.* 'Black Tulip' x *M.* 'Deep Purple Dream')
This is again a vigorous grower bred by Michael Gottschalk and flowered at Caerhays three years from planting. The flowers are globe shaped with wide tepals and a rich magenta-purple in colour. The young tree already has a spreading habit as you can see.

• *M.* 'Antje Zandee'
(*M.* 'Black Tulip' x *M.* 'Deep Purple Dream')
This is the same cross from the same breeder but is certainly good and different enough to merit its own name. While it is so difficult to find words to differentiate between magnolia

colours this is described as a 'dark purple-pink' in the Magnolia Society International Register and cherry-red-purple by the breeder himself. Our plant was planted out in 2014 and first flowered in 2018. It has an upright habit and smaller flowers than *M.* 'Aphrodite'.

The latest excellent introductions from New Zealand

• *M.* 'Burgundy Star'
(*M. liliiflora* 'Nigra' x *M.* 'Vulcan')
Originally known and patented as 'JURMAG4', this was bred by Mark Jury in 1993 but only patented in 2009. You would expect a special colour from these parents and 'Burgundy Star' certainly is. An upright habit and star-shaped flowers with dark violet tulip-shaped flowers that catch the eye even from a distance.

• *M.* 'Livingstone'
(*M. sprengeri* 'Diva' x *M.* 'Vulcan')
This was bred by Ian Baldick in 2013 and shown to us first in a slideshow at Burncoose during one of his UK visits. Its first flowerings here have shown how exceptional the red-purple tepal colours are. Our plant has an upright habit.

• *M.* 'Tikitere' (*M.* 'Apollo' x *M.* 'Vulcan')
Both parents are late-season flowerers and 'Tikitere' is one of the very last tree magnolias to perform each season from a young age. The cup-shaped purple-pink flowers are wind hardy and long lasting, often well into May. The tepals are darker outside and very light pink inside although the colour fades considerably as the flower matures.

Best new yellow-flowering magnolias
Over the past 10 to 20 years, we have been overwhelmed by the numbers of new yellow-flowered magnolia hybrids, which usually just manage to flower before their leaves emerge. While *M.* 'Lois', *M.* 'Green Bee' and *M.* 'Daphne' still take some beating, these two have performed especially well here.

M. 'Sweet Merlot'
(*M.* 'Sweet Simplicity' x *M.* 'Black Tulip')
Bred by Vance Hooper, the large, wide flowers have dark purple-pink outsides to the tepals, which are near white on the inside.

M. 'Honey Tulip'
(*M.* 'Yellow Bird' x *M.* 'Iolanthe')

This compact, slow-growing magnolia is absolutely splendid in May at nearby Burncoose House. The hybrid was patented under the name 'JURMAG5' in 2016. It was bred in New Zealand by Mark Jury and is now available in larger garden centres.

The numerous tulip-shaped yellow flowers appear in May and it has been described as the soft golden form of *M.* 'Black Tulip'. Magnolia growers in the west and south of the UK seem to have fared rather better with this plant than those in the north where it has, as yet, not performed as well.

• *M.* 'Ossie's Yellow'
(*M.* x *brooklynensis* x *M.* 'Miss Honeybee')
Although only registered formally in 2018, two plants of this variety have been performing well here for the past few years. The flowers do appear with the leaves but are a really striking yellow and numerous. It often has decent secondary flowers in the autumn as well. This variety is named after the New Zealand breeder who raised it, Oswald Blumhardt.

Newer magnolias with mixed colours in their flowers

These may, perhaps, not be to everyone's taste but there is no doubt that *M.* 'Peachy' and *M.* 'Daybreak' have gained in popularity recently because they offer an unusual colour combination and flower rather later in the season. There are other variations on this theme that are well worth growing. *M.* 'Honey Liz' and *M.* 'Judi Zuk' have been described in earlier articles and are becoming better known in gardens, however the four listed below are not as yet.

• *M.* 'Crescendo'
(*M.* 'Yellow Lantern' x *M.* 'Big Dude')
US bred by Dennis Ledvina and first recorded in the 2012 *Rhododendron, Camellia & Magnolia Group Yearbook*, this plant has tiny buds that open into huge flowers with a mix of pink, yellow and white in the tepals. The yellow is more pronounced on the outside of the tepals as the buds emerge and then fades.

• *M.* 'Hot Pants' (*M. campbellii* var. *mollicomata* x *M. sprengeri* 'Diva'?)

We grow *M.* 'Hot Lips' and *M.* 'Hot Pants' here, both raised from the same cross involving *M. sprengeri* 'Diva' at Herkenrode in Belgium. To us, 'Hot Pants', raised in 2016, is far the better colour mix as you can see (p47).

• *M.* 'Peaches 'n' Cream'
(*M.* 'Star Wars' x *M.* 'Yellow Bird')
The flowers each have six tepals, which are peachy-pink towards the base and white at the apex with hints of yellow as the flowers open. It was bred by Dennis Ledvina in the USA in 2013.

• *M.* 'Sunset Swirl'
(*M.* 'Daybreak' x *M.* 'Pink Royalty')
Admittedly this is my favourite of these new mixed-coloured magnolias. This one is a gentle mix of yellow, pink and eventually white on only the inside of the upright tepals. Bred by Dennis Ledvina in the USA in 2008.

Magnolias with blue buds

Who would have thought that 'blue' could be possible as a magnolia colour? Individual forms of *M. acuminata* ssp. *acuminata* demonstrate something really exceptional in the magnolia world is now possible. *M. acuminata* ssp. *acuminata* 'Blue Opal' is becoming more popular among Burncoose Nurseries customers but the following two are even better blues.

• *M.* 'Seiju' (syn. 'Blue Eternity')
This selection has iridescent blue-green buds opening to bright yellow inner tepals. We first saw it featured in an article on yellow magnolias by Koen Camelbeke from Herkenrode and were determined to add it to the collection.

Magnolias with exceptional scent

We are all used to the scents of magnolias but these three are particularly scented, often covered in insects, and need to be grown near a path to enjoy them fully.

• *M.* 'Rebecca's Perfume'
(*M. soulangeana* 'Amabilis' x *M.* 'Mark Jury')
The lily of the valley scent of the large flowers with thick, wax-like tepals can be detected from 10 paces away. The shiny white tepals have a pink-red base both inside and out. It was bred by Oswald Blumhardt and introduced into Europe by Michael Gottschalk.

• *M.* 'Woodsman' x 'Patriot'
As far as we know this cross has yet to obtain a registered name but it certainly deserves one. Our plant was planted in 2007 and soon started flowering. The colour range evolves spectacularly from the blue buds as you can see in the two photographs above.

• *M.* 'Scented Gem'
Recently acquired from Kevin Hughes Plants,

it was collected from a temple in South Korea by John Gallagher and is thought to be a form of *M. denudata*. Its scent is absolutely gorgeous and not at all like a 'normal' magnolia smell.

Dwarfs
- *M.* 'Mighty Mouse'

This is a dwarf and selected seedling form of the well-known and admired *M.* 'Genie' bred by Vance Hooper. It would be suitable for pot growing and would fit into the smallest garden. Like *M.* 'Genie' it is a profuse flowerer at a very young age but the dark purple flowers, and the tree itself, are tiny. An apt name!

New *Michelia* hybrids
Although taxonomists tell us we are not now allowed to call them anything other than magnolias, this merely serves to confuse traditionalists. The two shown are a small sample of the now perfectly hardy, extremely floriferous from a young age, and garden worthy *Michelia* hybrids which have appeared from New Zealand since 2013.

- *M.* 'Southern Belle'
(*M. sieboldii* x [*M. tripetala* x *M. obovata*])
Magnolia enthusiasts have come to know and admire the late-May-flowering 'Summer Solstice' (*M. obovata* x *M. globosa*). We think that 'Southern Belle' is even better. Our plant came from Eisenhuts' nursery in Switzerland in 2009 although it was, as its name implies, US bred. The flowers are huge and appear in June first with gorgeous pink outer tepals opening to reveal hugely scented white flowers with red stamens. It is making a big tree with a multi-stemmed habit and took eight years to flower properly. This contrasts to the 1992 planted 'Summer Solstice', which has a single trunk and is now 10.5m (35ft) tall. Its flowers are similar but rather smaller.

• *Michelia* 'Fairy Blush'
(**M.** *figo* x [**M.** *doltsopa* x **M.** *yuyuanensis*])
These plants are a spectacle and flower away
precociously for months even in pots. They
may ultimately develop into small trees but, as
pyramidical-shaped bushes in smaller gardens,
they take some beating. So far there are four
different-coloured 'Fairies' (Blush, Cream,
Lime and White) and all are equally good with
exceptional scent. Eight years from planting
out here our plants are around 3–3.5m (10–
12ft) tall with a spread of 1.2–1.8m (4–6ft).

• *Michelia laevifolia* 'Summer Snowflake'
Unlike *M. laevifolia* itself this form has much
larger pure white flowers that open out saucer
-flat to give a dazzling and lengthy display with
plenty of scent.

Cornish-bred hybrids
To recognise the work of Cornish magnolia
hybridisers, here are a couple of older and one
brand new selections. Improved grafting
techniques and more nurserymen now growing
magnolias means that some of the best older
named plants in Cornish gardens can now be
offered more widely.

• *M. campbellii* 'Peter Borlase'
This was introduced into circulation in 1989
by David Clulow but was originally selected by
Peter at Lanhydrock from nine other seedlings
in 1967. It first flowered at Lanhydrock in
1985. As you can see from this photograph of
our 2005 planted plant it is well worth its place
in any woodland garden and has a mixture of
colours in the same way as *M*. 'Betty Jessel'.
It is the last of the forms of *M. campbellii* to
flower here well after all the others.

• *M. campbellii* 'Elisabeth Holman'

This is one of Nigel Holman's finest magnolias that he raised at Chyverton. It deserves to be more widely grown and admired as we found when a 2014 planted plant first flowered in 2018. To us it appears to have *M.* 'Lanarth' in its parentage and the seedling was originally given to Nigel by Michael Williams of Lanarth.

• *M.* 'Martha Joan Leslie'
(*M.* 'Rose Marie' x *M.* 'Blushing Bride')

This was formally registered by Andrew Leslie in 2020 and has grown in his garden at Ethy House since 2007. It was originally a gift from Nigel Holman as a hand-pollinated seedling performed by John Galbraith. The flowers are enormous and a deep purple-pink at first fading to a lighter shade when fully open.

Inevitably this short article only skims through a few of the ever-growing number of new magnolias that are being grown here. One could equally easily write a similar article about 'poor' new magnolias (as they have performed here) or, on new hybrids that are pretty much identical to existing ones and not really worth the space – particularly true of yellow magnolias, of which far too many very similar plants, often from the same cross or seedpod, have been named and introduced.

Eisenhut's new book on magnolias lists and describes around 500 species and subspecies of *Magnoliaceae* (including *Michelia* and *Manglietia* and related semi-tropical species) together with around 1,050 named (and quite a few unnamed) hybrids. The Magnolia Society International checklist of cultivated magnolias currently lists around 1,603 named hybrids and cultivars. Relatively few of these have actually been formally and properly registered with the Magnolia Society International so the list inevitably has some duplicates where different breeders in different parts of the world may have sometimes undertaken the same cross.

I would guess that the number of magnolia hybrids and cultivars has more than doubled in the past 30 years so there are plenty more yet to try out in the collection here. In recent years, several new (to us) species of *Magnolia*, *Michelia* and, especially, *Manglietia* have flowered at Caerhays and Burncoose but perhaps that's a topic for another article.

Charles Williams VMH *is the current custodian of Caerhays Castle gardens and is senior partner of Burncoose Nurseries.*

Mixed blessings of rarity

Audrey Tam

John Gault is a rhododendron propagator who has run a nursery in Limavady, Northern Ireland, since the 1960s, specialising in species and hybrids that are sufficiently hardy for the north coast. Presently he is the only rhododendron breeder in Northern Ireland; even at the age of 88, his nursery propagates about 1,000 deciduous and evergreen azaleas, dwarf and hardy hybrids each year.

What is the worth of a plant?

At a time where emphasis is placed on measurable value, capitalistic wisdom suggests that whatever can be objectified can be monetised, leading to the belief that anything can be owned at the right price. Unlike real estate and luxury items, plants are affordable to more people, and the temptation to collect exclusive specimens is correspondingly higher – rare plant auctions are commonplace these days. But what about a specimen so rare, and the underlying relationship to the plantsman so intricate? Its worth is simply not quantifiable, and serious ethical considerations come into play regarding responsible guardianship and legacy conservation. In this article I will discuss one such example.

The discovery of 'Red Max'

In summer 2021 I had the opportunity of assisting Mr John Gault at his Rhododendron and Azalea nursery. As a first-year Cafre student of horticulture, it was an eye-opening experience and the perfect chance to discuss a wide range of botanical topics. As we were talking about genetic mutations in plants, Mr Gault handed me an article from the Summer 2020 issue of the *American Rhododendron Society* (ARS) *Journal* (Hyatt, 2020) describing a rare mutant variety of *R. maximum* called 'Red Max'. Contrary to the common variety that displays deep green lanceolate leaves and white (sometimes tinged pink) corolla (Cox and Cox, 1997), 'Red Max' has a red sap coursing through some of the foliage, staining some leaves dark red, bleeding from the mid rib towards the margin, and causing some buds to bloom red.

This exceedingly rare specimen was first sighted in the wild as a small cluster hidden deep in the woods near Mount Mitchell in North Carolina. Since its discovery in the 1930s, numerous excursions have been organised to inspect the cluster with the aim to preserve it and collect cuttings/seeds for propagation in cultivation. Sadly all the wild 'Red Max' specimens perished save one, and its location is now a closely-guarded secret.

Since it is almost impossible to root from cuttings, grafting and seeds are the only propagation method, preventing 'Red Max' from being introduced to the wider horticultural community. Adding to the complication, the origin of the red sap is still unclear and its distribution throughout each propagated specimen varies unpredictably, manifesting itself in each plant in different degrees, sometimes not at all, sometimes not for several years (Hyatt, 2020). 'Red Max' is the rarest of the rare, shrouded in mystery.

53

The original 'Red Max' in Mr John Gault's garden (photos taken June 2016), displaying that unmistakable red tinge to the foliage and similar flower variations as the *R. maximum* 'Mount Mitchell' seen in Mr Donald Hyatt's ARS article – *all photos:* **John Gault**

When Mr Gault handed me the ARS journal article, I took it as a case in point of genetic mutation in rhododendrons. Nothing prepared me for what Mr Gault said the next day, "I have the 'Red Max' in my garden". Unable to contain my excitement and curiosity, I hurried back to the nursery to inspect the plant. Tucked away in a corner, a juvenile specimen was growing slowly but already displaying that unmistakable, tell-tale crimson red sap in some of the young foliage; the drought in July seemed to have saturated the colours.

Mr Gault reckons that he acquired what is possibly the UK's only 'Red Max' by accident. About 20 years ago, he bought a seed batch of regular *R. maximum* through the Scottish Rhododendron Society, which is affiliated with the ARS. Among the 15 seedlings grown from the batch, one quickly emerged as an outlier: it grew at only half the rate but displayed a different, slightly red-tinged foliage colour. Gradually other seedlings were sold save for this one, and – 15 years after the seeds were first sown – the plant reached flowering age. The two flower buds opened with a red-white variegation, which was extraordinary – as

mentioned, the regular *R. maximum* variety displays white or pale pink flowers.

During 2016 the plant flowered much more profusely, again in the same unusual colour variegation. Recognising that he had received a rare sport, Mr Gault tried in vain to propagate it by cuttings but succeeded in grafting a stem onto a *R.* 'Cunningham's White'. The timing for the graft proved fateful: during peak flowering season the following summer, the original plant died overnight, which to this day remains a mystery because environmental conditions had been normal and no other plant in its proximity had suffered in the same way. Fortunately the grafted plant grew on happily, and it is the one and only specimen that Mr Gault has today. The recent drought of July 2021 didn't seem to affect its health; on the contrary it is displaying even more of its signature blood-red foliage especially on the young growth. Interestingly, Mr Gault didn't realise what he had in his possession until the 2020 ARS article was published, when he compared photos from the article with the specimen in his garden and recognised, with a fair bit of excitement and pleasant surprise, that it is a 'Red Max'.

So far Mr Gault hasn't come across any other 'Red Max' owner in the UK. In the interest of knowledge exchange and botanical legacy preservation he hopes to speak with other 'Red Max' owners, and for this reason asked me to write this article. He welcomes anyone who is interested to reach out via his email: **jlandmaureen@aol.com**

The price of rarity

Making the decision to share his story has not been easy; the main concern is that it might attract the unwanted attention of trophy hunters misguided in the conviction that anything in this world can be bought at the right price. But how is one to price a plant that doesn't only deliver visual impact and the 'wow' factor, but has the potential to further our understanding of genetic mutation in rhododendrons? What about the ARS' decade-long effort to preserve it for posterity, or the anguish Mr Gault experienced at the death of the original seedling, which took 15 years to grow to maturity?

Casting aside the rarity factor, the sentimental bond a plantsman develops with a plant that he painstakingly nurses from seed, and which takes anything from five to ten years to flower, can be difficult to quantify in money terms. I am reminded of a touching passage in the ARS article, when the author considered how the 'Red Max' on Mount Mitchell escaped a recent wildfire unscathed: 'I could see where flames had been within a few feet of the trunk, but miraculously, I saw no sign of damage! How that fire managed to avoid this rare specimen still baffles me! All I could think of is that the spirits of past great Rhododendron leaders like Joe Gable, David Leach, Augie Kehr, Ed Collins, Bob Stelloh, and other admirers over at least the last half century must have gathered round to deflect the flames.' (Hyatt, 2020)

For a plant that is so rare and presents so much scientific promise, it would be a great shame if an environmental disaster wipes it out from existence. But equally it would be a heartbreak to see it languish in the uncaring, inexperienced hands of someone who believes that, with a deep enough pocket, he or she can buy the world.

The grafted 'Red Max' clone in its current stage of growth (August 2021). The July drought and bright sun brought on stronger foliage colours

REFERENCES

Cox, P. A. and Cox, K. N. E. (eds) (1997): *Encyclopedia of Rhododendron Species,* Glencarse: Glendoick Publishing.

Hyatt, D. W. (2020): The Mystery of the 'Red Max', *American Rhododendron Society Journal,* 74(3) pp156–161.

Audrey Tam *is a second-year Foundation of Horticulture degree student at the College of Agriculture, Food and Rural Enterprise. Born and raised in Hong Kong, Audrey moved to Northern Ireland four years ago and has developed a passion for gardening, despite having to be content with extremely unfavourable environmental conditions in her back yard.*

The Palm Valley Nursery Company of Guangzhou, China and the ever-blooming camellias

Brenda Litchfield

On the outskirts of Guangzhou City, Guangdong Province in southern China, just north of Hong Kong, is an exciting nursery that is the centre of the camellia world for breeding year-round, continuous-blooming camellias. They have now produced 508 year-round-blooming camellias.

Background to the nursery

The Camellia Breeding Base is part of the Palm Landscape Architecture Company Ltd, established in 1984. The parent company has several departments: Landscape, Gardening, Nurseries, Design and Research with more than 3,000 employees and many large nurseries in different parts of China. The Camellia Breeding Base encompasses 500 acres (203ha) and has three sections: the parent area for creating crosses, the hybrid area for cultivating hybrid seedlings and the propagation area.

The Camellia Breeding Base was set up in 2006 under the direction of Dr Gao Jiyin, who had retired from his job at the Research Institute of Subtropical Forestry, Chinese Academy of Forestry, Fuyang, Zhejiang and went to work full-time at the Palm Landscape Architecture Company in 2005. He has been involved in researching and growing camellias for more than 50 years and his work includes research into oil-producing camellias, camellia species, the introduction of exotic camellia cultivars and, most significantly, the breeding of a new generation of camellia varieties that can produce flowers all year round.

He was instrumental in setting up the new and important Camellia Species garden at Jinhua, which was created for the International Camellia Society (ICS) Congress there in 2003. He also co-wrote *The Collected Species of the Genus Camellia: An Illustrated Outline*, with Dr Clifford R Parks and Dr Du Yueqiang, introducing more Chinese species to the Western world; the book was written in Chinese and English and was published in China in March, 2005. It includes descriptions for 199 species and the photographs alone broke new ground.

In 2016, he published the book *Illustrations of the New Camellia Hybrids that Bloom Year-round*, also written in both languages. This book published by Huayu Nature Book Trade Company in China introduced 323 new camellia varieties including 217 new *Camellia azalea* hybrids with a year-round blooming trait, and 55 *C. amplexicaulis* hybrids with an extended blooming period.

When Dr Gao visited the site of the discovery of *C. azalea* (syn. *C. changii*) in 2000 and saw it blooming in summer and at other times of year he immediately recognised the importance of its potential commercial viability for breeding all-year-round blooming camellias. Over the years he has published several articles for both the American Camellia Society (ACS) and the *ICS Journal* about his hybridising work with *C. azalea* and

C. amplexicaulis, which is the other year-round flowering species he has used to create summer-flowering and potentially year-round-flowering hybrids.

The purpose of the Base is to create new hybrids in a wide range of colours, unusual flower forms and different sizes of flower that bloom in summer or year-round. I find their achievements to date amazing.

Dr Gao has given me his most recent breeding figures, which are 508 year-round blooming camellias and 724 new camellia varieties, of which 20 new varieties have been introduced to the market; 323 crossed combinations and 120 successful combinations with more than 200,000 crossed cultivars have been made, yielding in excess of 5,000 hybrid seedlings. There are 327 *C. azalea* F1 and 181 F1 back-cross hybrids.

Dr Gao's selection of new hybrids (left to right):

Top Row: C. 'Xiameng Yueting' ('Mrs. Yue Ting's Summer Dream'); C. 'Siji Caibao' ('Four Seasons' Treasure'); C. 'Guangchang Wuhui' ('Dancing in Square'); C. 'Xiari Hongyang' ('Summer's Red Sun')

Middle Row: C. 'Jinqiu Meigui' ('Roses in Autumn'); C. 'Kuoban Fenshang' ('Broad-petal Pink Skirt'); C. 'Majuan Nsühi' ('Mrs. Ma Juan'); C. 'Guichang Xiansheng' ('Mr. Guichang')

Bottom Row: C. 'Hongtian Xiangyun' ('Red Sky with Fragrant Cloud'); C. 'Xiameng Wenqing' ('Mr. Wenqing's Summer Dream'); C. 'Xiari Baota' ('Summer's Pagoda'); C. 'Zhuchun Xiumei' ('Scarlet Lips & Charming Eyebrows')
– *photo*: **Dr Gao Jiyin**

Camellia 'Siji Cabao' ('Four Seasons' Treasure')
is a hybrid of *C. japonica* 'Jinpan Lizhi' × *C. azalea*
– *photo*: Dr Gao Jiyin

The author with *C. azalea* trees – *photo*: Gao team mem

He and his team have bred 101 hybrids of
C. amplexicaulis, but there are also 33 normal
camellia hybrids and 82 normal camellia
varieties from chance seedlings. I believe the
hybrids with their ever-blooming trait
represent a revolution in the camellia world.

In Chinese conditions these hybrids grow
strongly and sprout new shoots three to four
times a year because the two main parent
species are semi-tropical plants with
asynchronous shoot development. The
Chinese recommend planting the hybrids in
full sun for maximum blooming and a well-
developed root system. Because they grow fast
and bloom year-round, they require more
nutrition to reach their full potential, so
fertilising is important on a regular basis. The
ever-blooming hybrids have certainly changed
the expectation that people have had for a
thousand years about the normal timings for
flowering being from autumn to spring.
Currently, more than 20 authorised nurseries
in China propagate the camellias from the
Breeding Base under the control of Chinese

patent rights. It is estimated that there are in
excess of 3 million hybrid potted plants
beautifying landscapes and households in
China. With this background about the
nursery and its hybrids, I can now describe
my visit to this amazing research site.

Visit to the nursery

I had heard about Dr Gao's breeding work
through the ACS and, with the help of ACS
members, I contacted him to arrange a visit
while I was teaching at universities in Macao
(once a Portuguese colony and also a semi-
autonomous area, like Hong Kong) and Xi'an
in China. I was privileged to visit twice and
was picked up at the train station by Dr Gao
and two of his research team members. Our
first stop was to visit the retail nursery of the
Palm Landscape Architecture Company in
Guangzhou. Almost all the plants there are
C. azalea in every size you could imagine up
to huge trees. This is where the plants from
the research station are sent for distribution
throughout southern China.

Medium-sized *Camellia azalea* trees – Brenda Litchfield

Location and climate

The Palm Valley Nursery is about 30 minutes from the city through rice fields and past many duck and fishponds. The roads are concrete so travelling is easy. The climate is subtropical and Guangzhou is rated as Zone 10b – the same as Melbourne, Australia. The hot season lasts for nearly six months and temperatures range from 34°C (91°F) to a low of 27°C (80°F). The cool season lasts for two to three months; temperatures stay above 9°C (48°F) and the average January maximum is 18°C (65°F). Humidity is high from May to October and rainfall is abundant especially in summer, with around 1,700mm (68in) annually. These are easy growing conditions for camellias.

I stayed on site, so I was able to meet the dedicated, enthusiastic, young research team working with Dr Gao. They are all college educated, mostly in biology and botany, and regularly receive visitors from all over the world to their attractive, purpose-built site and take pride in showing them the nursery and all the unique, new camellia hybrids.

Parent species

The primary cross-parents that have been used in the breeding programme are *C. azalea* and *C. amplexicaulis*. The deep red flowers and thick, narrow leaves of *C. azalea* and the unusual bloom structure and large quilted leaves of *C. amplexicaulis* have produced some amazing hybrids to date.

Most of the hybrids start to bloom from mid-summer, then fully bloom from autumn to winter and continue blooming but a little less strongly in spring. The hybrids grow vigorously and flower in full sun in summer temperatures of 37°C (100°F) and can grow normally in winter with air temperatures of -2°C to 0°C (28–32°F).

All the hybrids of either species are disease-resistant, and no *Ciborinia camilliae* (camellia petal blight) has been found in the hybrids so far. Many of the hybrids also have the unique and amazing trait of producing up to ten buds on a stem (pictured on p61). Because they have thick leaves they show good resistance to chewing bugs.

Camellia azalea was a chance discovery from 1984, named by Professor Wei Zhaofen of the South China Botanical Research Institute in 1986. The few shrubs, bordering on extinction, were found on the banks of a small river in Guangdong Province, southern China. It is now rated "critically endangered" in the wild. In *Collected Species of the Genus Camellia* authored by Gao, Parks and Du, it states on p34 that "in preliminary tests it has survived -5°C". *Camellia amplexicaulis* (Pitard) Coh.St. (1916) is now considered extinct in the wild and was placed on the IUCN Red List of Threatened Species and classified as endangered in 2018. In *Collected Species* on p23, we learn that *C. amplexicaulis* originates from the border of Vietnam with the Chinese province of Yunnan and has been cultivated as an ornamental plant in Vietnam for many years.

C. amplexicaulis has purplish-red incurved flowers and very large dense leaves up to 25cm long. The base of the leaf clasps the stem, hence its name, which means just that. The blooming season is mainly summer and autumn, but under controlled conditions it can bloom year-round. It has limited capacity to withstand cold, but can tolerate a few degrees of frost. *C. amplexicaulis* seemed a possible parent for breeding new cultivars that bloom through several seasons, and some now do.

Dr Gao writes in his 2016 book that both species show some variation in form. *C. amplexicaulis* can have a thin white edge to its flower or a white double flower in similar style; *C. azalea* has wide, narrow and wavy petal forms, and sometimes a more erect flower or more wax-like petals. Dr Gao commented about hybridising with these two species in 2005, "Hybridisation, so far, has worked well with Japonicas, Williamsii and Reticulatas but not Sasanquas. Some of the most interesting flowers have been produced by the hybrids of *C. amplexicaulis*."

More are being produced each year by the research team: one of the surprising results mentioned in Gao's 2016 book is the light yellow seedling 'Huangchoudan' ('Yellow Satins') off *C. japonica* 'Tama Beauty' where *C. amplexicaulis* is the male parent. Originating from the same cross is *C.* 'Caihuang' ('Colourful Yellow'), a new cultivar with a fascinating flower (see p61).

Dr Gao with his research team – *photo:* Brenda Litchfield

Multiple bud set appears on most hybrids

Camellia azalea flower – *photos*: Brenda Litchfield

C. amplexicaulis flower – *photo*: Bradford King

C. amplexicaulis leaves – *photo*: Brenda Litchfield

C. 'Huangchoudan' ('Yellow Satins')

C. 'Caihuang' ('Colourful Yellow')
– *photos:* Dr Gao Jiyin

Nursery tour

We began my tour of the site in the seedling area. Hundreds of thousands of seeds are planted each year in raised beds of sand bordered by bricks. Each one is then carefully potted up to be used mainly as root stock or perhaps a new variety. They are planted in pots when they are about a year old and remain there for another year. Then they are moved to a larger growing area and planted in the red soil in small mounds.

Next, we moved to the large hybrid section of the nursery where many different varieties are crossed with *C. azalea* and *C. amplexicaulis*. Each of the thousands of crosses is labelled meticulously and covered with a net bag to prevent further pollination. When the seeds are ripe, they are picked and taken to the hybrid greenhouses for further processing. In one of the greenhouses, hybrid seeds are

Camellia seedlings in sand

Dr Gao with the newly potted seedlings

Older potted seedlings

Two-year-old seedlings planted in mounds of soil – photos Brenda Litchfield

arranged by the parent used in the cross and carefully monitored through the initial stages of their growth in this protected environment. They are checked regularly, and research notes are carefully logged regarding growth. Quite a bit of grafting also takes place in the greenhouses. Using the abundant rootstock, scions from successful hybrids are grafted for faster growth and blooming.

After one to two years in the greenhouse, the young plants are planted anywhere and everywhere. So much for planting in improved soil or with mulch! This was perhaps the biggest surprise for me. Everywhere I looked there were camellias planted in the red soil. They were on slopes, in between palm trees, on the sides of roads and in just about every available space that could be used. And they were all thriving in this environment. Even with 500 acres (203ha), there is still a space

Net bag covering ripening seeds

Harvesting carefully crossed, labelled ripe seeds

Potted hybrid seedlings

Older hybrid seedling camellias –
photos: **Brenda Litchfield**

problem. So when they ran out of room for the potted camellias, they simply drained a lake to make more land available.

Most of the plants in the lake area were 'Red Leaf Bella' and *C. azalea* in canvas bags with what appeared to be just normal soil from the area. These will eventually be used for hybrid crosses with various parent plants, and some are used for grafting. The number of plants is absolutely astounding and stretches as far as the eye can see in every direction.

Seedlings are planted out in every available space including on slopes

Potted camellias filling a recently drained lake
– *photos*: **Brenda Litchfield**

The discovery of 'Red Leaf Bella'

'Red Leaf Bella' is an exciting Chinese mutation of *C. japonica* 'Nuccio's Bella Rossa' discovered by Fu Bingzhong in Jinhua. Dr Gao describes in the *ACS Journal* winter 2009/10 how it arose after scions were grafted in 2002 onto fast-growing *C. japonica* 'Hongluzhen' [1993 China], which is highly resistant to virus. The plants thrived and were used to graft an additional 100 plants, then another 500 plants. That is when the red leaves appeared on one of the grafts! Those leaves were grafted and maintained their colour over four years and through 5,000 grafted plants. There are now more than 10,000 'Red Leaf Bella' plants in eastern China.

Dr Gao says it is thought that the mutation is a result of a chromosome being broken during grafting. This unique mutation has caused quite a stir in the camellia world because the new leaves are a beautiful deep purple with bright green markings. Older leaves change to almost a purple bronze colour. Because they all exhibit different patterns and changing colours, the plants look absolutely spectacular.

The new plant was named 'Hongye Beila' in 2006 and it has the western synonym 'Red Leaf Bella'; its other Chinese synonyms are 'Bella Jinhua' and 'Jinhua Meinü'. The plant

The author with *Camellia* 'Red Leaf Bella'
– *photo*: **Gao Team member**

The stunning foliage of *Camellia* 'Red Leaf Bella' (top and above)

Large *C. gauchowensis* plants (top) and close-up of a graft (above) – *photos*: **Brenda Litchfield**

has reached America but may still be subject to quarantine controls and I am told it is already being grown in Spain from where it may have been exported elsewhere.

There is now another beautiful mutation from 2009 with red leaves and red flowers with many white spots or patches called 'Hongye Huabeila' with the western synonym of 'Red Leaf Bella Variegated'. Both mutations are strong growers.

Grafting

Another large part of the Camellia Breeding Base focuses on grafting. Oil-producing camellia *C. gauchowensis* is the preferred grafting stock for camellias at the nursery. Distinguished in 1961 by Chang as a separate species, it originates in Guangdong province

and it is preferred for several reasons. It grows remarkably quickly and has proven to have the best compatibility with grafts. As a result, the grafts grow quickly and all have a high survival rate. Small plants, large trees and also the roots can be used, which provides a lot of options for grafting. Plus there is an abundance of these plants in southern China so they are less expensive.

Some of the seedlings they grow are grafted onto rootstocks and thousands of grafts are made each year. They graft small plants grown in canvas bags as well as huge plants that are more than 6m tall. The best grafting method is using very large trees, on which all the branches and leaves are cut off. Then they wait for all the new shoots to emerge from the trunks and the grafts are made in the tender,

Multiple grafts are made on each rootstock – *photo*: **Brenda Litchfield**

The author signing 'The Book' – *photo*: **Gao Team Member**

The author planting C. 'Xiari Guanghui' ('Summer's Sheen') with Dr Gao – *photo*: **Gao Team Member**

new shoots. The grafts are wrapped with thin plastic, which remains until the scions break through and begin their growth. Often a large tree of *C. gauchowensis* can have more than 100 grafts. When the grafts take and the growth is stable, these large trees are dug up and shipped to landscape companies for use in developments, cities and homes in China.

Dr Gao's grafting method has been followed in other countries. Rather than grafting directly into rootstock that has been cut off several inches high, he cuts the rootstock, waits for it to sprout several sprouts and grafts into them. It is easier because only a razor blade is needed rather than a saw. Each rootstock may produce several shoots so the resulting plant is thicker with more leaves. You can find a detailed explanation and photographs of this excellent method as well as other types of grafting on the website of the American nurseryman Gene Phillips from Savannah, Georgia (**https:// genesnursery.com**).

Visitors to the Camellia Breeding Base sign 'The Book' and plant a commemorative plant to celebrate the visit. I was certainly surprised that my special planting area was only about 4.5m (15ft) from the edge of the lake. After always hearing about not letting camellias get wet feet, I was interested to see how my plant would grow in such a wet environment. When

C. oleifera **seed-processing room on the ground floor of the building** – *photo*: **Brenda Litchfield**

C. 'Xiari Fenqun' ('Summer's Pink Dress')

C. 'Hongtian Xiangyun' ('Red Sky with Fragrant Cloud')

C. 'Xiari Qixin' ('Summer's Seven Hearts')

C. 'Siji Xiumei' ('Four Seasons' Beauty')
– *photos*: **Dr Gao Jiyin**

I returned the next year, my plant of *C. azalea* hybrid 'Summer's Sheen' (Xiari Guanghui) was taller than me! This attests to the fast growth rate of the new hybrids being developed there. They grow twice as fast, and produce two to three times as many blooms as *C. japonica* plants. This is because most are grafted on *C. gauchowensis*, which is such a strong, fast-growing species. In his 2016 book Dr Gao says of 'Summer's Sheen' that "older leaves will change to orange-red to red after autumn" – a very unusual trait for a camellia! – and he includes a photograph that is also in the Register.

Camellia oil from *C. oleifera*
On the ground level of the main building at the nursery is a large room where women workers, who earn about 50 cents or pence a day, sit on tiny stools for hours and sort and dehusk seeds of *C. oleifera* for making camellia oil. This fine oil is used in many cosmetics as well as cooking in China. About 25% of Chinese people use camellia oil as their main cooking oil. Because it is a 90% unsaturated oil, it is even better than olive oil. So nothing is wasted at the nursery.

Sharing new hybrids with the world
Dr Gao encourages nurseries and camellia organisations around the world to work with him to develop these exciting hybrids. He wants to share all his work and knowledge with camellia enthusiasts, nurseries and

Camellia 'Zonglin Xianzi' ('Fairy in Palm Forest')

C. 'Xiameng Yulan' ('Mrs Yulan's Summer Dream')

C. 'Xiameng Xiaoxuan' ('Miss Xiaoxuan's
Summer Dream' – *photos:* **Dr Gao Jiyin**

growers, and can be contacted at
y25006@163.com.

The first country to receive hybrids was
Australia. After 2016, the new hybrids were
sent to Holland, France, Spain, Portugal, Italy
and Japan. Preliminary reports were, and still
are, overwhelmingly positive about their
growth and blooming in these countries.

After several years of US plant quarantine,
a few selected growers in the US are
extremely excited to have received six
different varieties of the Chinese ever-
blooming hybrids, including 'Hongwu Jixiang'
('Scented Deposition from Red House'),
which the Camellia Register shows is a cross
of *C. azalea* × *C. japonica* 'Kramer's Supreme',
a scented cultivar that has passed on its scent;
'Guichang Xiansheng' ('Mr Guichang') from
a cross of *C. azalea* × *C. japonica* 'Bob Hope',
is in the Register, saying "Blooms mainly in
summer, autumn and winter and sporadically
in spring"; 'Xiari Qixin' ('Summer's Seven
Hearts') (photo p67) is registered as a peony
form cross of *C. azalea* × 'Dr Clifford Parks'
from 2011, flowering from "summer to
early winter"; and 'Xiameng Xiaoxuan'
('Miss Xiaoxuan's Summer Dream') is a
seedling of *C. azalea* × *C. japonica* 'Daikagura'
with pink, double, especially beautiful flowers
with 38 petals (photo bottom left), and is
also photographed in the Register.

Additionally, the American Camellia
Society has registered three of the Palm
Landscape Company's hybrids in 2021, which
are all described as flowering "summer to
winter – continuous". They are 'Mrs Yulan's
Summer Dream' ('Xiameng Yulan'), which is
a cross of *C. japonica* 'Miyakodori' × *C. azalea*
and is a striking red "single with 6 inter-
arranged magnolia-like petals" as can be
seen in the photograph (centre left);
second, 'Summer's Wind and Hot Waves'
('Xiafeng Relang'), which is a pink semi-
double to loose peony form with 37 petals
and some deep red veining visible and is a
cross of *C. azalea* × *C. japonica* 'Daikagura';
last, 'Mr. Wenqing's Summer Dream'

('Xiameng Wenqing') has a red anemone to full peony form flower and is a cross of *C. azalea* × *C. reticulata* hybrid 'Dr Clifford Parks'. All can be found in the Camellia Register together with photographs.

Two *C. azalea* hybrids have even been ACS registered from US breeding in Cairo, Georgia, USA by Pat B Johnson and both are also said to bloom from summer to winter continuously since 2015. 'Mark C.' is a "deep, dark red – small single" and a hybrid between *C. japonica* 'Scarlet Glory' × *C. azalea*. 'Mark C.' has the additional feature of a bronzy to burgundy-coloured juvenile leaf as is seen in the photograph (right). 'William Khoury' has a crimson semi-double flower and is from a cross of a seedling of *C. japonica* 'Scarlet Glory' × *C. azalea*.

Finally, I have learnt that *C. azalea* hybrid '1001 Summer Nights Jasmine' originally from Palm Landscape is being grown in the UK. It is being kept inside as a young plant but is also being tried outside in Surrey and Cornwall as a bigger plant. It also has the multiple bud set, which is the special feature of these hybrids and makes for such exceptionally floriferous plants.

Everyone at the Camellia Breeding Base was a delight to meet. I learned a great deal about all their work with the new, ever-blooming camellias and I hope to return in the future to see what else they have added to the camellia world.

C. **'William Khoury'**

Camellia **'Mark C.' flower** (above) **and new growth colour** (above centre) – *photos*: **Pat B Johnson**

ACKNOWLEDGEMENTS

My thanks go to Bradford King and Pat B. Johnson for their photographs and also to Dr Gao Jiyin for his kind provision of photographs and information.

Brenda Litchfield *is a retired university professor and a co-author with Forrest S. Latta of* The Camellia Garden Field Guide (2015)

Magnolia sinostellata

Erland Ejder

Magnolia sinostellata (above and far right) – *all photos*: **Erland Ejder**

"Take heed that ye despise not one of these little ones;"(Matthew 18:10, *King James Bible*, 1611)

There has always been an interest in small-growing magnolias for small gardens, but this has become ever-more relevant as woodland gardens become increasingly rare. Lionel de Rothschild was credited with once opening a lecture to city gardeners with the now famous statement: "No garden, however small, should be without one or two acres of rough woodland". As amusing then, no doubt, as it is today.

Among the less tall-growing magnolias, *M. stellata* is a favourite, supplemented by *M. liliiflora* and hybrids between the two: the 'eight little girls'. Not that any of these is a rock garden plant but can still be counted among reasonably small-growing trees/shrubs. However, *M. stellata* can reach about 10m tall, with a 50cm stem diameter, which I saw

for myself in Gifu province in Japan!

Another member of the smaller brigade is the subject of this article: *Magnolia sinostellata*. In my garden I have a group of several different clones of this species, all grafted on *M. kobus* stock and after 12 years they are still below 2.5m tall, except for one stretching up another half metre.

Distribution

M. sinostellata was first described scientifically in 1989 from plants found at Caoyutang Forest Farm in Jingning County of Zhejiang Province in China. No doubt the plants must have been well known to local people much earlier but not brought into the spotlight. However, it has been reported that over the years a considerable number of these magnolias have been dug up and sold as attractive garden plants. More about conservation later.

Zhejiang is one of the easternmost

provinces of China, with a coastline on the East China sea, south of Shanghai. Intuitively one rather associates magnolias with the more wildly mountainous Chinese landscape further west. Although Zhejiang province lacks these towering mountains, there is plentiful terrain above 1,000m altitude, even approaching 2,000m, with ample precipitation and some frost and snow in winter – so the existence of a *Magnolia* flora is not very surprising. Also, we should bear in mind that, in mid-Japan, there are *M. stellata* populations down to just 10m above sea level in a really warm climate. Several references and comparisons to Japan's *M. stellata* distribution will be made later.

The first discovery and description of *M. sinostellata* as a new species was at Jingning as noted before, but gradually more populations have been found in other places in the west, mostly southwest (within a radius of about 50km) of the same province, in all about six localities with a possibility of some more awaiting discovery. The population sizes are reported as 'number of clumps' as it is obviously often difficult to disentangle the number of clones in places where regeneration by root suckers from established plants is common. Population sizes are roughly 300 down to two 'clumps'. In total about 600 plants (clumps) have been found and there is a chance that some more might be found. In this respect the situation reminds of the *M. stellata* distribution in Japan. Admittedly, there are many more populations in Japan but they are often very restricted in size and scattered over a limited geographical area of three prefectures, Mie, Aichi and Gifu.

Whether *M. sinostellata* has once been much more widespread in the general area where it is now found is open to speculation. There has been a hunger for farming land in China for a long time and even more so during the fast population increase after 1950. Marginal land has been brought into cultivation as is seen all over China and a reversion has not started to happen until recent years. Zhejiang is well known for high quality tea and rice production

and even small patches of land in mountainous regions have been used. Both *M. sinostellata* in China and *M. stellata* in Japan are mostly found in swamps, at the edge of streams or otherwise moist soil locations. The question whether this is the result of evolution or just a last refuge in competition with other vegetation has never been researched, but these ecological niches have the advantage of giving the plants more light than would be possible under the canopy of stronger-growing competing vegetation. At least for *M. stellata* there is an obvious change in plant height from individuals a little inside

Magnolia stellata on the left and *Magnolia sinostellata* on the right in both images above

the forest's edge to the position in the adjoining marsh where the ground is totally soaked in standing water. Both species have proven in cultivation to be able to grow well in normal soil with no water surplus, but those who have a wet spot in the garden might be interested in trying a plant of *M. sinostellata*.

The attractiveness of this plant for garden cultivation was obvious for a long time, and it has been reported that for many years plants were dug up and sold, or simply removed so as not to compete with agricultural crops. This is of course serious for a rare species like *M. sinostellata* but fortunately a praiseworthy conservation project has now been put in place, of which more later.

Description

The botanical description of *M. sinostellata* is as follows:
A shrub, (1.0-)1.5-3.0(-6.0)m. Bark grey. 1–2 year old twigs green with no or sparse hair. Leaf shape narrow elliptic to obovate (egg-shaped, narrower at the basal end) oval, 7–12 x 2.5–4cm. Leaf apex (tip) acuminate (tapering to a slender point) or caudate-acuminate (tail-like-). Leaf base cuneiform (wedge-shaped). Leaf hair: upper surface

glabrous (smooth without hairs), lower surface glabrous or with soft white hair along the midrib (and veins). Leaf surface sunken along veins. Flower diameter 5–7cm. Tepal number (9)12–15(18).
Tepal shape: No sepaloid tepals, same form of exterior and interior tepals, oblanceolate (inverse lanceolate [like a lance head, pointed at the tip]) or obovate-spatulate (egg-shaped, narrower at the basal end – spatula-shaped), 2.8–5.1 x 1.2–2.4cm, apex (tip) round or subacuminate (almost pointed). Tepal colour pink to light red, white, or only red in mid-lower or along the middle abaxially (outside of the tepal). Stamens 7–10mm, light pink or ivory yellow. Gynoecium (innermost whorl) cylindrical, 0.6–0.8cm. Fruits cylindrical, 4–6cm. Distribution: Jingning, Songyang and Wenzhou counties, Zhejiang province, China. Elevation 700–1,200m.

Several of these characters are illustrated above.

Species status

The definition and description of new species is a constant problem in botany. Variation in nature is immense. Some botanists, 'the splitters', want to describe new species based on small and perhaps insignificant differences from an established species. Others, 'the lumpers', accept more variation within a species and thus fewer species with a broader spectrum of differences in characters.

The taxonomic validity of *M. sinostellata* was not widely accepted at first. There are obvious similarities to *M. stellata* and in *Flora of China*, *M. sinostellata* was placed under *M. stellata* as a synonym. This was a majority decision within the author group and with the comment "Naturalised in Zhejiang (Jingning) [native to Japan]." This would mean that it would have been brought into cultivation from Japan and spread, forming a population in Zhejiang province. This suggestion now seems most improbable as more populations have been found and analysed and as a thorough investigation into similar and dissimilar characters between the two species have been made. The reasons now available for seeing *M. sinostellata* as a species in its own right are mainly the following.

A species always has an area of distribution. In this case the present distributions of *M. sinostellata* and *M. stellata* are separated by 2,000km, mainly sea. This might seem reassuring, but in a wide evolutionary perspective it can be interpreted in a different way. The east China Sea between Japan and China is not deep, in the order of 100m. During earlier geological epochs much more water was locked up in glaciers, and it has been shown that there was a land bridge between what is now Japan and the present east coast of China about two million years ago. The two floras have been shown to have surprising similarities. The time span might seem enormous but then we should consider that the evolution of *Magnolia* stretches over tens of millions of years. So, even if the overall assessment is that *M. sinostellata* and *M. stellata* should now be seen as separate species, their evolutionary history can be connected, explaining the considerable shared characters. However, during a subsequent very long isolation it is quite normal that the two populations have drifted apart. This can be caused both by random evolution and by different selection forces. So even if *M. sinostellata* and *M. stellata* have a common, similar ancestor, it is quite reasonable that they should now be seen as two different species.

In addition to the often-mentioned *M. stellata*, *M. amoena* (of eastern China,

Magnolia sinostellata **showing considerable variation in flower colour**

not very well known) has been considered as perhaps related to *M. sinostellata* and thus worthy of a detailed comparison. *M. cylindrica* and *M. denudata* are also found in Zhejiang province but as they have other chromosome numbers (tetraploid and hexaploid, respectively) they are very distinct even if populations of them might exist in the same geographical area. *M. sinostellata, stellata* and *amoena* are all diploid. In order to make a thorough comparison and decision of species status it is very useful to study different kinds of criteria of these three (supposedly distinct) species.

Morphology is the size, shape and structure of a plant. *M. amoena* is a higher growing plant, more treelike than the other two. Also, it lacks the sepaloid tepals of *M. sinostellata* and has a constant number of nine tepals.

M. stellata has brown twigs with more or less short hairs and sepaloid tepals in contrast to the other two species.

Pollen: the size, shape and surface structure is a highly special branch of botany. Pollen grains of the three species have been studied under Scanning Electron Microscope and show obvious differences between them.

Cytological comparisons have also been made. During meiosis (the pre-process of creating pollen and ovules) the chromosome behaviour in pollen mother cells can be studied in detail. In addition to chromosome counts, irregularities leading to reduced pollen fertility can be identified. *M. sinostellata* and *M. stellata* – but not *M. amoena* – display considerable such irregularities, which is consistent with few, small, fractured populations.

Nowadays, it is also possible to directly study the DNA sequences of selected chromosomes. Results from such investigations have largely shown identical sequences but there are about ten substitutions between the three species in question. From the detailed analysis a close relationship but reasons for separate species status can be inferred.

In conclusion, *M. sinostellata* can defend a position as a good taxonomic species, probably with a closer relationship with *M. amoena* than with *M. stellata*. So, for the foreseeable future we will have *M. sinostellata* on our taxonomic *Magnolia* palette.

Conservation

Many magnolias of the world must unfortunately be regarded as threatened in their natural habitats. Reasons vary, but mostly they are due to habitat loss from large-scale forestry and increasing farming land area. The Red List of *Magnoliaceae* paints a sad situation of different degrees of precariousness.

The situation of *M. sinostellata* is a perfect example and the situation was soon realised by Chinese botanists who embarked on an ambitious conservation project between 2015 and 2017. One of the project leaders was Dr Wang Yaling of the Xi'an Botanical Garden and I have had several opportunities to hear about this project from her.

A key idea has been to engage the local people at the few natural populations instead of just protecting, shutting off and forbidding. By appealing to the pride and joy of having something beautiful and worthwhile in or close to the village, teaching about it and organising how to make it valuable as a small business in a sustainable way – long-term success seems possible.

The name of the project is 'Conservation of genetic diversity of *Magnolia sinostellata* and reintroduction in its native habitat, SE China'. The project goal is stated:

'To enhance the success of propagation techniques for this species and implement a series of training courses for representatives from local communities and forestry agencies to strengthen horticultural skills. This will form the basis for *ex-situ* conservation and reinforcement programmes for wild populations in later years.'

To accomplish this goal, project objectives are:

• 'To improve the natural regeneration ability and [increase] individual numbers in their natural habitat; The Forest Farm can get some profit from tourism and get more financial support for protection.'

• 'To promote its utilisation in local landscape. Two or three varieties will be [selected] out for gardening purpose [over] the project duration.'

• 'To improve local farmers' livelihood by training them to cultivate and breed those varieties.'

The project has also been supported by non-Chinese organisations, the BGCI (Botanic Gardens Conservation International) and the Franklinia Foundation. As a result of this project, it has been reported that several field investigations have been made, the known populations characterised in detail and a few new ones found. Methods of seed sowing, rooting of cuttings, grafting and stooling propagation were explored and in the order of 10,000 saplings (mostly seedlings but also many grafts) have been produced and used for reinforcement plantings.

'More than 100 technicians from the forest farms were trained on how to identify, propagate and monitor *M. sinostellata*.

'They paid more attention to this species, including setting up protected areas, improving habitats by providing sufficient lighting conditions to improve its viability. Signboards were erected near localities where some rules of endangered species [were] illustrated.

'Three clones of *M. sinostellata* resulting from artificial crossings have been selected, grafted and will be used for landscaping.'

Propagation

My own more limited experiences of propagation of *M. sinostellata* are encouraging. Chip budding in late summer or early autumn on *M. kobus* or *M. acuminata* is easy – although the thin twigs carrying the growth buds demand some extra manual dexterity.

Semi-hardwood cuttings, treated in a quick dip of 5,000ppm indole butyric acid in 50% ethanol, 50% water, readily produce roots. I have only done this on an experimental scale

Magnolia sinostellata

Magnolia sinostellata

because there has been no need for many plants, but also partly because I always have problems overwintering newly-rooted cuttings in a cool climate and have limited protection structures.

A plant species that forms clumps in the wild can be suspected to be easily vegetatively propagated. Artificially or accidentally layered branches of *M. stellata* have a good tendency to produce new vertical shoots from the ground from buried buds in addition to common root formation on the layered stem and this applies also to *M. sinostellata*. I have successfully tried *M. sinostellata* propagation by trench layering as a method to get grafted plants to produce new plantlets on their own roots. At the buried resting growth buds, both a shoot develops upwards through the shallow soil covering and roots are forming downwards at the same stem node.

Seed propagation is, surprisingly, not as straightforward as might be expected. When fertile seeds are produced, they can be handled like any other magnolia seed. I keep them at about 4°C for three months in lightly moist sphagnum moss (not peat) in the refrigerator before sowing. However, seed production is very low.

In my garden it would be tempting to just blame the problem on cool spring weather and occasional night frost. The situation is more complicated because low seed production is also a problem in the natural populations in China. Small, isolated populations are often generally said to be at risk of inbreeding depression: the accumulation of deleterious genetic mutations causing decrease of fertility. This seems to be the case in *M. sinostellata* and actually some cytological studies have been made of the detailed process of meiosis, the start of seed formation. Inversion mutations were found, which means that a piece of a chromosome is broken off and inserted again "the wrong way around". It often causes disturbance in chromosome recombination and the formation of empty pollen grains.

This is the background that explains why plants from hand-pollinated natural seed from different populations have recently been planted into existing populations, they are 'fortified' in order to get a wider genetic base and increased seed production in the future. The idea seems useful, at least as long as normal genetic traits having evolved locally and naturally are not obscured.

I have indeed raised a limited number of viable *M. sinostellata* seedlings from seed in my garden without problems. A hybrid between *M. sinostellata* and *M. stellata* has flowered but not found to be of special garden merit. Further hybridisation with *M. sinostellata* might be of interest, although pollen production is low and arduous to collect.

Hardiness
During the past 12 years when I have cultivated several *M. sinostellata* plants in my garden I have had no winter hardiness problems, and although they flower early in spring, they have suffered very little frost damage. The flowers are of course not immune to such calamities but seem to have above-average frost resistance, at least as developing flower buds.

Conclusion
M. sinostellata is a very attractive garden plant. It is easy to cultivate, develops quickly without growing excessively tall, and branches out readily. The habit is graceful, the leaves are decorative and characteristic and the flowers are quite pretty, presented in masses. Adding that *M. sinostellata* is easily propagated, it can indeed be recommended for widespread cultivation.

Availability of plants is a problem at present but the situation will hopefully improve. A few plants of *M. sinostellata* were offered in the Burncoose Nurseries catalogue in 2009 under the name 'China Town' (syn. 'Jing Ning'). I have often seen one of these plants, which was sent to Sweden, and it looks like a true *M. sinostellata*. It means a few *M. sinostellata* should be growing somewhere in UK gardens. They obviously originated from some Chinese wholesale nursery, but details are obscure. A plant from Bulk Nurseries of The Netherlands was also imported about the same time under the name 'China Town' but was not *M. sinostellata* but *M. stellata* or a hybrid.

In case of emergency, I would be willing to supply graftwood to enthusiasts in need.

ACKNOWLEDGEMENTS

My thanks to Dr Wang Yaling of Xi'an Botanical Garden for sharing information and material of *M. sinostellata* with me over many years.

REFERENCES

Markings for references have not been inserted in the text of this article. The two main sources of information – in addition to my own practical experiences – are the following:

Wang Y-L, Ejder E, Yang J-F, Liu R, Ye L-M, He Z-C, Zhang S-Z. 2013. *Magnolia sinostellata and relatives (Magnoliaceae). Phytotaxa* 154 (1):47–58.

BGCI. *Conservation of genetic diversity of Magnolia sinostellata and reintroduction in its native habitat, SE China*. Unpublished project report. 2018.
(A short abstract is available at https://www.bgci.org/our-work/projects-and-case-studies/integrated-conservation-of-magnolia-sinostellata-zhejiang)

Erland Ejder *is a retired physicist living in Sweden and a member of the Swedish Magnolia Group. He has travelled in China and Japan, mainly for Magnolia studies.*
erland.ejder@telia.com

Harewood House
The development of the Rhododendron Gardens, and early hybridisation in North Yorkshire: an historical perspective

John M. Hammond

Aerial photograph of Harewood House looking north and its surrounding formal gardens and wide vistas of parkland, which contain a collection of specimen trees – *photo*: **Harewood Estate Trust**

The Harewood estate was created in its present size by merging two adjacent estates, the Harewood Castle estate based on Harewood Castle itself, and the Gawthorpe estate based on the Gawthorpe Hall manor house. The properties were combined when the Wentworths of Gawthorpe, who had inherited that estate from the Gascoignes, bought the neighbouring Harewood estate from the Ryther family. The combined estate was subsequently sold to the London merchant Sir John Cutler in 1696, after whose death it passed to the Boulter family. They in turn sold it to the Lascelles family in 1739.

In the late 17th century, members of the Lascelles family had purchased plantations in the West Indies, and the income generated allowed Henry Lascelles to purchase the Harewood estate in 1739; his son, Edwin Lascelles, 1st Baron, who was a wealthy plantation owner, built the house between 1759 and 1771 to replace Gawthorpe Hall; the original manor house, coach house and stables on the estate were to be demolished and their location was to disappear beneath a large lake during the laying out of the designed landscape.

Edwin Lascelles initially employed the services of John Carr, an architect practising in the north of England, previously employed by a number of prominent Yorkshire families to design their new country houses.

The foundations were laid in 1759, with the house being largely complete by 1765. The fashionable Robert Adam submitted designs for the interiors, which were approved in 1765. Adam made a number of minor alterations to Carr's designs for the exterior of the building, including internal courtyards. By the spring of 1758, Lancelot 'Capability' Brown had been involved with providing rough sketches of the proposed designed landscape to Robert Teesdale, the Head Gardener at Harewood, and was later chosen by Edwin to landscape the grounds.

When Brown eventually arrived in 1772, he dammed Gawthorpe Beck, a relatively small stream, to create an extensive lake of 32 acres (12 hectares) and hid the view from the house of the water entering the north end of the valley and leaving at the south end, to flow into the River Wharfe a mile away. Brown was absent for long periods of time after work had commenced, leaving a neglectful supervisor to take the project forward, which created many problems, so that Edwin found himself apparently in charge at times of a major project on his own lands. Edwin delayed

payment of Brown's invoices until agreement was reached for the necessary remedial work to be carried out to correct poor workmanship. As a result, Brown took eight years to complete the enormous landscape, planting clumps and circling belts of trees, to give the impression that land rolled away smoothly from the walls of the house to the far distance and arranged that the Pleasure Garden was located well out of sight of the vistas from the house.

Despite the practical difficulties of transforming such a vast area of land, Harewood remains one of the finest examples of Brown's genius and his way of turning rough, hilly countryside and farmland into a vista of 'natural' beauty. One of his obsessions was to plant yew and beech trees to hide unsightly buildings, and over the years they eventually formed a dense canopy, which prevented later planting of shrubs. Meanwhile, the remnants of the original Harewood Castle are still extant and can be found contained behind the sharp corner of the estate wall 460m to the north of the main entrance to the estate on the A61 Leeds to Harrogate road.

Capability Brown dammed the valley to form a lake and introduced the Cascade with a bridge across the outlet at the west end that becomes Stank Beck, flowing into the River Wharfe – *photo:* **John Hammond**

The house remained largely untouched until the 1840s when Sir Charles Barry, architect of the House of Commons, was employed by Henry Lascelles, 3rd Earl of Harewood, the father of 13 children, to increase the accommodation. Barry added second storeys to each of the flanking wings to provide extra bedrooms, removed the south portico and created formal parterres and terraces. From 1843–1848, Barry created a large terrace in front of the house with three ornamental fountains, balustraded walls and statuary, his work directed by Lady Louisa Thynne, 3rd Countess of Harewood. Barry left the floral infilling of the beds to John Fleming, Head Gardener. Sir Charles Barry's Italianate terraces at Harewood became a national standard around the mid-century and were reflected in many country house gardens.

Henry Lascelles was born in 1846 and as a child lived at Goldsborough Hall, which was the house for the heirs-in-waiting for Harewood House, and during his lifetime the Lascelles family were still major landholders in Barbados. He initially served in the regular army as captain in the Grenadier Guards, after which he served part-time as an officer in the Yorkshire Hussars Yeomanry, which became part of the Territorial Army in 1908. He was lieutenant-colonel in command of that regiment from 1881–1898 and honorary colonel from 1898–1913. He succeeded to the titles of 5th Earl of Harewood, Viscount Lascelles on 24 June 1892. He also held the post of colonel and yeomanry aide-de-campe to Queen Victoria from 1897, Edward VII throughout the latter's reign, and to George V from 1910 until his own death.

During 'The Great War', between 1914–1918, Henry offered the use of Harewood House as a convalescent hospital for officers wounded in action, which was accepted by the Red Cross and attached to the 2nd Northern General Hospital in Leeds. The family retained the East Wing, which was conveniently sealed off with its own staircases and provided with a temporary kitchen, as the main kitchen was required by the hospital staff. Of necessity, the

Sir Charles Barry created the large terrace in front of Harewood House between 1843 and 1848 with three ornamental fountains, balustraded walls and statuary, leaving the floral infilling of the beds to Head Gardener John Fleming – *photo*: **Harewood Estate Trust**

Kitchen Garden was completely turned over to food production, while a separate 8-acre (3.2 hectare) field was allocated to the Head Gardener Harold Hall. Harold, who had become Head Gardener as recently as 1912, having moved from Lathom Hall across the border in Lancashire, had around 20 staff, many of whom were specialist growers in their own right for supplying particular food for the kitchen and flowers required for the house, which included grapes, figs and all kinds of fruit, carnations, orchids and chrysanthemums in the heated greenhouses, while salad and vegetable crops were raised in the Walled Garden, together with flowers to be cut for the house.

Commensurate with the way unmarried garden staff were accommodated and learnt their trade in the years prior to WWII, they lived at Harewood in a communal rustic brick 'bothy', which was located close to the Walled Garden and greenhouses on the south side of the lake, just about as far away as was practicable from the house and a 20-minute walk from the Courtyard. They were looked after by a 'bothy woman' who cleaned up the bothy and cooked meals.

The Walled Garden is the oldest garden on the estate, being already under construction when building of Harewood House began in 1759. With specially designed buildings and hothouses for growing exotic plants and food crops, together with twelve huge beds utilising 1 acre (0.4 hectares) of the area within the Walled Garden and resembling a communal allotment. Until around 1750 the Kitchen Garden would usually be located close to the house, as its purpose was to provide the kitchens there with the finest fresh fruit and vegetables, so it was readily accessible to the kitchen staff. With the growing trend for the house to be set amid a designed landscape and be surrounded by formal gardens, the Kitchen Garden was banished to a remote location and hidden from view; and of necessity needed to be provided with tall walls to provide adequate shelter from the incessant winds. However,

the estate now needed sufficient gardening staff and at least eight staff would have been employed full-time in the Walled Garden, while an 'improver' (a lad in training) would have taken the produce up to the house.

Harold Hall would have only just got to grips with the food production cycle, expectations of the kitchen staff, preparation of flowers for the house and maintenance of the grounds, when war was declared with Germany and major changes were essential. Crops now needed to be raised to support the soldiers and nursing staff in the hospital, as well as the Earl and his family, together with the estate workers. The eight-acre (3.2 hectare) field was put down to growing interplanted rows of potatoes and sprouts, and, as labour was cheap, the Head Gardener and staff were remitted to grow more produce than was required, so the residue could be taken to Leeds market by horse-drawn wagon and be sold, which contributed towards the cost of growing the food.

The future of the family lay with the 5th Earl's eldest son, also called Henry, who after education at Eton College, attended the Royal Military College, Sandhurst, before being commissioned as a second lieutenant into the Grenadier Guards on 12 February 1902, serving until 1905. As a result of his father's 'connections' he became an honorary attaché at the British Embassy in Paris from 1905–1907, then served as aide-de-camp to the Governor General of Canada, Earl Grey, until 1911. After the outbreak of the First World War he re-joined the Grenadier Guards for service on the Western Front in April 1915 and was wounded in the head at the Second Battle of Givenchy but recovered to fight in the Battle of Loos in 1915 and was wounded a further two times as well as being gassed. He was promoted captain and later major in command of the 3rd Battalion in 1915, and lieutenant-colonel in 1918. He was awarded the Distinguished Service Order and a bar in 1918, as well as the French Croix de Guerre.

In 1922, Henry Lascelles the 6th Earl

married Princess Mary, the only daughter of George V, which was a major step in securing the future of Harewood House and its grounds. Meanwhile, the 5th Earl had begun to restore Harewood House after the evacuation of the hospital had taken place in 1919, but the economic climate did not permit anything beyond the necessary repairs and restoration caused by its wartime use. The 5th Earl passed away in October 1929 and Henry Lascelles and Princess Mary made detailed preparations to move from the nearby Goldsborough Hall into Harewood House, which led to many improvements being made to the house and gardens to make it more suitable for them. In 1930 the couple moved permanently into Harewood House in the midst of the alterations being taken forward by the York-based architects Messrs Brierley & Rutherford. In 1932 King George V gave Princess Mary the title 'The Princess Royal', and Harewood House became a royal residence. Queen Mary would pay an annual visit in late summer, leading to great pomp and circumstance.

Early rhododendron hybridisation in North Yorkshire

The Honourable William Herbert, third son of Henry, 1st Earl of Carnarvon at Highclere Castle, descended from the Earls of Pembroke and Montgomery, was born in January 1778. In 1814 he was presented to the Rectory of Spofforth, five miles south of Harrogate in North Yorkshire, by his relative Colonel Wyndham and became Rev William Herbert with a living of £1,600 a year, which he held up to his death on 28 May 1847. Herbert was among the earliest in Britain to study hybridisation on a large scale; and while he was particularly interested in the *Amaryllidaceae*, he did not limit his experiments to these or to bulbous plants. He had an extensive garden at Spofforth and in 1817 he produced the first rhododendron hybrid by crossing two species (*R. viscosum* × *R. maximum*) to create the *Azaleodendron*

R. 'Hybridum', dark purple in bud and opening to rosy-lilac, paling to white in the tube, with a ray of yellowish-green markings.

There has been considerable discussion for many years as to the circumstances that led to the blood-red form of *R. arboreum* first flowering in spring of 1825 at 'The Grange', Northington, Alresford in Hampshire, the estate of Alexander Baring. For seedlings of *R. arboreum* to have been grown on to flowering stage in 1825 the seed must have arrived in Britain around 1810, given that it takes about 15 years for *R. arboreum* to begin to flower.

Dr Francis Buchanan (1762–1829) was a product of the University of Edinburgh's Department of Medicine, and trained as a surgeon, who then joined the East India Company's establishment in Bengal in 1794 as a surgeon, but in common with many of his calling, he had a keen interest in collecting botanical specimens.

His family hailed from the Leny Estate in the Callander district of Perthshire. He became friends with Dr William Roxburgh, a very knowledgeable botanist on the plants of Northern India, who in 1799 recommended him Lord Wellesley, then Governor-General in Bengal, as 'the best botanist he knew in India', which led to Buchanan's appointment as Wellesley's surgeon.

Buchanan surveyed Nepal during 1802–3 and, after accompanying Wellesley back to England in 1806, he returned to India and in 1807–1809 surveyed in detail parts of West Bengal (now Bihar) and North Bengal. During this period while stationed on the borders of Nepal he collected seeds of blood-red *R. arboreum* and sent them home in 1809 or 1810, some being passed to the Royal Botanic Garden Edinburgh.

Thus, Buchanan is attributed as being the first to introduce the species and when Lindley figured and wrote-up the first flowering in cultivation at 'The Grange' in the *Botanical Register* Vol.XI (1825), it was suggested that the plant was likely to have

This deep pink hybrid in the Rock Garden (top) has all the characteristics of a *R.* 'Naomi' clone from the cross of *R.* Aurora Group × *R. fortunei* made at Exbury in 1926. The deep pink, lax, frilly flowers with crimson markings in the throat and shiny obovate leaves (above), suggest this may be *R.* 'Naomi Pixie', a clone not often seen in cultivation. In 1932 Lionel de Rothschild began sending plants to the 6th Earl of Harewood when the rhododendron collection was initially being established – *photos*: John Hammond

Raised from seed sown in 1956 of a *R*. 'Loderi King George' cross, this hybrid has fragrant white flowers with a rose-coloured blotch in the throat. It is tall, reflecting its Loderi heritage and has long shiny leaves

come from seed sent by Buchanan to the Royal Botanic Garden Edinburgh, some being forwarded to Alexander Baring at 'The Grange'. The first man to hybridise with *R. arboreum* was James R. Gowen, a gentleman of independent means, who in 1826 on behalf of the Earl of Carnarvon, obtained a truss of the plant at 'The Grange', carefully packed and carried it in a tin box back to Highclere, where pollen from the truss was crossed with an unnamed hybrid (*R. catawbiense* seedling × *R. ponticum*) to produce the hybrid *R*. 'Altaclerense', which flowered in 1831.

As one of the earliest and very active hybridisers, it is highly likely that William Herbert, son of the Earl of Carnarvon, also had access to the *R. arboreum* truss when it arrived at Highclere Castle in 1826 and made his own cross of *R*. 'Nobleanum' (*R. caucasicum* × *R. arboreum*), using this in his further hybridisation work. Being a Whig, and a supporter of Lord Melbourne's

Government, he was appointed by the Crown to the Wardenship of Christ's College, Manchester, on the death of Dr Calvert, and was installed, on 10 July 1840, becoming Dean of Manchester, then elected a trustee of Bury Grammar School in 1841. In the midst of this he made many other rhododendron and azalea crosses including (*R. caucasicum* × *R*. 'Nobleanum') in 1835, with bright pink flowers edged in red and red spots in the throat, later becoming known as *R*. 'Jacksonii'; the name is thought to have been derived from the same cross made c1845 by W Jackson & Co of Bedale in Yorkshire. *R. caucasicum* had been sent to the Royal Botanic Gardens, Kew and was introduced in 1803, but never became common in cultivation.

Spofforth Rectory was but five miles northeast of Harewood House, so William Herbert would have been known to the Lascelles family and *R*. 'Nobleanum' with bright rose red flowers duly arrived at Harewood and remained a family favourite across the generations, together with a good form of the bright rose-pink *R*. 'Jacksonii'. These hybrids can be found beyond the terrace adjacent to the sloping lawns to the west of the house leading to the gate into the parkland. It also should be noted that the beautiful hybrid narcissi raised by William Herbert at Spofforth are illustrated in the *Botanical Magazine* (1843), and many groups are planted at Harewood. Herbert gave great attention to raising new varieties of daffodils, and it is to him we owe the hundreds of beautiful narcissi that now adorn our gardens.

While the vast grounds of Harewood had been laid out by 'Capability' Brown, whose work created the much-admired splendid views, and despite the 5th Earl's passing liking of rhododendrons, including the bright rose-red *R*. 'Nobleanum', which flowered in late winter or early spring, Harold Hall, his Head Gardener from 1912–1953, was given very little scope for planting more ornamental shrubs in the years following The Great War.

Establishing Harewood's major rhododendron collection

As well as having an interest in racehorses, the 6th Earl was very fond of rhododendrons, so in 1932 he sought the advice of Sir William Wright Smith, Regius Keeper at the Royal Botanic Garden Edinburgh, with the intention of establishing a rhododendron collection in the grounds. In liaison with Harold Hall, Sir William initiated a significant rhododendron planting programme. Specimen plants were sent from some of the most famous stately homes in Britain, no doubt resulting from the Earl's discussions over dinner with various estate owners recommended by Sir William, which was how things had been done since Victorian times. Rhododendron personalities including Lionel de Rothschild, Sir Gerald Loder, Lord Aberconway and John and Roza Stevenson helped start Harewood's collection.

Planting commenced in the woodlands in 1932 with plants sent by Lionel de Rothschild from Exbury, including the somewhat rare R. 'General Sir John du Cane' (R. *thomsonii* × R. *fortunei* ssp. *discolor*), named after a famous WWI soldier, with rose-madder flowers and a dark crimson flash in the throat, which Lionel was particularly fond of and named and registered in 1933. This planting, in a large group near the greenhouses on the southwest side of the lake, includes R. 'Loderi King George' from Leonardslee, and R. 'Polar Bear' from Tower Court, which was one of the Princess Royal's favourites. It flowers in late July or August, and was regularly visited by both the Princess Royal and Princess Alice of Athlone when she was staying at Harewood. Another favourite of hers, planted in 1933 in the same group and still flowering at Harewood, was a R. *wardii* hybrid named after the famous plant collector Kingdon Ward. There are other yellow hybrids in the plantings at Harewood, attributed to W.C. Slocock, of Goldsworth Nursery, who made many crosses with R. *wardii*, and this unregistered hybrid probably came from the same source.

Sir William Wright Smith not only acted as a facilitator to source both species and hybrid rhododendrons, but also gave guidance regarding where to plant the various species and hybrids, taking account of the protection needed from the sun, wind and frost. While Harewood suffers from early frosts, the locations chosen by Sir William have tended to mitigate the level of damage expected in Yorkshire and many plants perform better than would be generally expected.

The Walled Garden was extensively refurbished in the 1930s, with modern glasshouses replacing most of the old hothouses, while the restoration of the house, which had been on-going throughout the 'interwar' years, had only just been completed when war broke out in 1939. Once again during WWII the house acted as a resident convalescent hospital for wounded soldiers and the family again retained the East Wing for their use. Following the cessation of hostilities and the evacuation of the hospital, a second renovation of the house was needed. The 6th Earl died in 1947 before he could undertake this onerous task, which was devolved to his young heir George Lascelles, 7th Earl of Harewood. His Majesty King George VI gave the Princess Royal a flat in St James's Palace, but Harewood House remained her home where she took an interest in the gardens and their upkeep. From 1950 onwards the family opened the house and gardens to the public and held concerts connected with musical establishments, including the Yorkshire Symphony Orchestra and Leeds Musical Festival, the latter of which the Princess was Patron.

On 28 March 1965, the Princess Royal suffered a fatal heart attack while walking the grounds of Harewood with her eldest son, the 7th Earl and his children, which left everyone on the estate stunned. She was 67 and was buried at Harewood Church. Continuity with her musical interests was maintained by her elder son, the 7th Earl, who was director of the Royal Opera House and later the English

Rhododendron 'John Waterer' (above left) is an early Waterer cross (*R. catawbiense* × *R. arboreum* ssp. *arboreum*) with slightly frilled scarlet flowers lightly spotted brown. Its rough-textured leaves hint to the days when nurserymen were experimenting with newly-introduced *R. arboreum*. To find it at Harewood House (above right) walk down past the stables, on the path running alongside the Lakeside Garden. *R.* 'John Waterer' is rarely mentioned but is found in many old gardens, including the Royal Botanic Garden Edinburgh where it was in cultivation prior to 1860.

Many rhododendrons in the Lakeside Garden are attractive crosses made by Geoff Hall, Head Gardener from 1953–1979, including this plant (above left) that attracts the attention of many visitors. Large multi-stemmed *R. thomsonii* (above right) graces the walk along the lakeside and a considerable number of species and hybrids can be seen along the south west side of the lake – *photos*: John Hammond

R. campanulatum with its lavender-blue flowers can be found in the Rock Garden close to the outlet of the lake along with *R. lutescens*, *R. fictolacteum*, *R. strigillosum* and many more – *photo*: **John Hammond**

National Opera; nearer to Harewood, he was a member of the Leeds Music Festival's Executive Committee and a patron of the Yorkshire Symphony Orchestra's concerts.

The next major step in developing the rhododendron collection was in 1953 when Geoffrey Hall succeeded his father Harold Hall as Head Gardener. Geoff Hall's formal introduction to rhododendrons began when he was a student at the Royal Botanic Garden Edinburgh and from this period sprang a life-long interest and a burning desire to saturate the northwest side of the lake with many new hybrids of his own breeding. Geoff started a breeding programme in 1956, crossing species rhododendrons, then harvesting the seed, germinating the seed and raising hybrids.

In due course, six new hybrids were registered with the Royal Horticultural Society, including *R.* 'Patricia Harewood', a 1959 cross (*R.* 'General Sir John du Cane' × *R.* 'Loderi King George') with cherry-pink buds leading to strong purplish-pink flowers suffused deep purplish-pink externally, and produced a beautiful small tree that Lord Harewood registered in 1979. Another hybrid was *R.* 'Lord Harewood', raised from seed sown in 1956 from *R.* 'Loderi King George', with white flowers and a rose-coloured blotch in the throat. Named and registered by Lord Harewood in 1987, it is found halfway along the southwest side of the lake.

Finally, Geoff named a hybrid after himself, *R.* 'Geoffrey Hall', crossed in 1959, parentage unknown, registered in 1988, blooms early May, flowers funnel-shaped, strong purple with a white tube in bud, opening strong purple paling to white in the tube with a small black-crimson blotch at the base.

Senior members may recall the 1962/1963 winter as being the coldest within living memory, when snow swept in on Boxing Day, depositing deep drifts across many parts of Britain, while the severe frosts lasted until early March. What has been generally forgotten is that disaster had already struck on Sunday 11 and Friday 16 February 1962, when two major storms caused massive damage to property and gardens across the central belt of Yorkshire. At Harewood the hurricane-force winds destroyed large areas of woodland, huge gaps appeared in the landscape and the density of the yew and beech canopy was significantly reduced, allowing parts of the estate to see the sun for the first time in 200 years. Repetitive destructive storms with only five days between them is most unusual, and investigations at the time suggested that the worst-case scenario was a five-year interval, while the 'norm' would be somewhere around 60 years. Thousands of mature trees were uprooted, as was the case when the Great Storm hit southeast England on 15 October 1987. Many trees crashed on top of each other like matchsticks, smothering the rhododendrons beneath; the scene in the

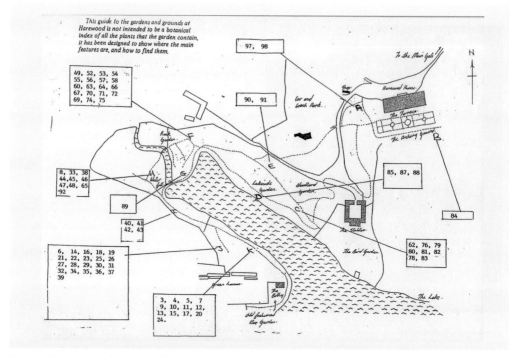

This guide to the gardens and grounds at Harewood is not intended to be a botanical index of all the plants that the garden contain, it has been designed to show where the main features are, and how to find them.

Harewood Plan The 7th Earl provided a plan of the garden areas that contain rhododendrons, which dates from 1995 – Harewood Estate Trust

1 'Cynthia'	no details	**37** Harewood Hybrid	**55** No details	**74** 'Bow Bells'
2 *R. dichroanthum* Hybrid	**18** No details	**38** 'General D. Eisenhower'	**56** 'Elizabeth'	**75** *R. wightii*
3 'Goldsworth Beauty'	**19** 'Pictum'	**39** *R. augustinii*	**57** 'Apple Blossom'	**76–85** No details
4 *R. chasmanthum*	**20** 'Britannia'	**40** 'Souvenir de Doctor S. Endtz'	**58** 1936 Gift	**86** 'Alice'
5 *R. rubiginosum*	**21** Unnamed	**41** 'Doncaster'	**59** 'Humming Bird'	**87** Harewood Hybrid
6 'Loderi King George'	**22** 'General Sir John du Cane'	**42** *R. concinnum* Hybrid	**60** *R. concinnum* Hybrid	**88** Original rhododendron
7 Harewood Hybrid	**23** 'Shilsonii'	**43** *R. yunnanense*	**61** No details	**89** *R. magnificum*
8 'Moser's Maroon'	**24** 'Polar Bear'	**44** 'Blue Diamond'	**62** 'Cynthia' type	**89a** 'Palestrina' (Az)
9 Hybrid, no details	**25** *R. fortunei* Hybrid	**45** *R. chaetomallum*	**63** *R. decorum*	**90** *R. vernicosum*
10 Hybrid, no details	**26** 'Fiona Wilson'	**46** 'Loderi' cross	**64** 'Irene Hall'	**90a** *R. cinnabarinum*
11 *R. albrechtii*	**27** 'Patricia Harewood'	**47** 'John Walter'	**65** *R. griersonianum*	**91** *R. davidsonianum* as *charianthum*
12 'Strategist'	**28** *R. vaseyi*	**48** Harewood Hybrid	**66** 'Gomer Waterer'	**91a** 'Pink Pearl'
13 Harewood Hybrid	**29** *R. dichroanthum*	**49** 'Lamplighter'	**67** 'Naomi' Hybrid	**92** 'Purple Splendour'
14 'Naomi' seedling	**30** *R. litiense*	**50** *R. ponticum* self-seeded	**68** *R. williamsianum*	**93** No details
15 Hybrid, no details	**31** No details	**51** *R. thomsonii*	**69** 'Coreta'	**94** 'Jacksonii'
16 *R. wardii* Hybrid	**32** *R. searsiae*	**52** No details	**70** No details	**95** *R. arboreum*
17 Hybrid,	**33** 'Mrs G. W. Leak'	**53** 'Sappho'	**71** *R. campanulatum*	**96–99** No details
	34 'Lord Harewood'	**54** *R. barbatum*	**72** *R. glaucophyllum* ssp. *glaucophyllum* (as *glaucum*)	
	35 Harewood Hybrid		**73** *R. racemosum*	
	36 Harewood Hybrid			

aftermath was unbelievable with 200-year-old oaks completely uprooted and left lifeless; indeed, two centuries of growth on the estate were lost over two nights of mayhem.

After the timber merchants had removed what timber was of value, the estate staff were left with some devastated areas to clean up, while many uprooted specimen trees had fallen into the lake and were submerged. These had to be winched out, hundreds of massive root plates had to be blasted and broken-up, then carted away, and the craters filled and levelled with soil from old tips on the estate. All this restoration work took a great deal of time to achieve and over the following years the opened-up areas provided space for a major replanting programme.

The 7th Earl acknowledged that the estate could only continue to be maintained by a sizeable portion of public money being raised by permitting visitors to view the house and grounds, as well as being supported by a considerable amount of his own income, so he was in the business of marketing his assets to survive and needed to attract public interest to make the project a viable proposition.

Geoff Hall retired in 1979, leaving very few records of the names and positions of the rhododendrons, and was succeeded by Alan Mason, well known as the Yorkshire TV gardener, who planted some modern dwarf rhododendron species. When Ian Powell took over as Head Gardener in 1988, he was faced with the daunting task of preserving and cataloguing the Harewood Rhododendron Collection. Fortunately, the cataloguing was resolved with the assistance of Michael Thorp, a 17-year-old student, who worked with Geoff Hall. As Geoff spent many hours going round the grounds and recording the history of each plant on a tape recorder, Michael transferred this onto a computer database and the collection was fully catalogued. Each plant was numbered, photographed and all the information linked into the database.

Many years ago, a start was made to label the plants and trees, but sadly the project was abandoned as the labels were removed, broken or thrown in the lake by the public. Around 1995 the 7th Earl supplied a map identifying the main locations where the 100 most interesting rhododendrons were planted, together with the names of the numbered plants (see left). This list is by no means exhaustive because the collection of 50 plantings in the vicinity of 'The Dell' also contained the brilliant crimson *R. strigillosum*, primrose yellow *R. lutescens*, suede undercoated leaves of *R. fictolacteum*, together with *R. rubiginosum*, *R. williamsianum*, *R.* 'Temple Belle' and many interesting smaller species suited to the rock garden.

Restoration work on the terrace in front of the house took place in 1994, with financial assistance from the European Union as Charles Barry's original elaborate flowerbed designs had been grassed over in 1959 because they were too labour intensive to maintain. When Trevor Nicholson took up the post of Senior Gardener on the estate in 1994 he was remitted with establishing the newly-renovated Terrace Garden, and his work met with the approval of the 7th Earl, so a year later he was promoted to Head Gardener. Trevor has introduced many rhododendron species during the creation of Harewood's Himalayan Garden, a redevelopment of the 'Rock Garden' nurtured by Princess Mary and her husband, the 6th Earl in the 1930s; it is an extraordinary world in miniature, a plant-hunter's paradise. With paths through a gorge and a bridge across the beck, this is a place for all garden-lovers to visit, with primulas, orchids, cobra lilies and blue *Meconopsis* to complement the rhododendron plantings.

Harewood won a Large Visitor Attraction of the Year award in the 2009 National Excellence in England awards. Harewood has more than 100 acres (40 ha) of gardens, and in 2004 David Lascelles, the 8th Earl of Harewood with a lifelong interest in Buddhism, invited a group of monks from Bhutan to construct a 7.5m high stupa, a hemispherical Buddhist memorial shrine, in the vicinity of the Himalayan Garden. It was important to the Earl that the stupa was built correctly, which in turn had its problems because the monks had never been outside the Himalaya and did not speak English. Lama Sonam, a Bhutanese master stupa builder agreed to come to England with his two assistants and build the stupa assisted by Yorkshire craftsmen to dress the local stone under the supervision of the Lama. It took four months to construct and fill the internal chambers with religious artifacts, then bless to the Lama's satisfaction. In 2005 the Lama and his two monks returned for the consecration of the stupa, attended by 200 guests including Prince Charles.

Harewood House is still the family seat of the Lascelles family, and home of David Henry George Lascelles, the 8th Earl, a 70-year-old film producer, who succeeded his father on 11 July 2011. Transferred into a trust ownership structure, managed by Harewood House Trust, the house and grounds are open to the public for most of the year.

In conclusion

The growing of rhododendrons continues to be a tradition at Harewood and each successive generation of the family has contributed to the collection and some specimens are survivors from the original collection, started by the 6th Earl in the 1930s. Very little has been written specifically about the Rhododendron Collection, so the above account has been collected from a wide number of sources mainly related to the house itself, as is Mary Mauchline's detailed history, listed in the references. In the 1960s and 70s the 7th Earl's interest in hybrids led to many colourful additions. Recent planting in the Himalayan Garden has extended the collection with species from China and the Himalaya. There are well over 100 different mature rhododendrons growing beneath the trees and along the margins of the lake.

As was the case from when the grounds were first opened to the public, visitors are encouraged to explore the gardens for themselves. Harewood is a particularly attractive garden to visit in spring and as the plantings are unlabelled, the accompanying map identifying the main locations where rhododendrons are planted, together with the list of the names of the numbered plants dating from the mid-1990s is a useful guide when visiting the garden.

Harewood House Terrace following its restoration in 1994 – the original flower bed designs had been grassed over in 1959 because they were too labour intensive to maintain – *photo*: **Harewood Estate Trust**

To complement the Himalayan Garden, Harewood Head Gardener Trevor Nicholson introduced a stupa, a hemispherical Buddhist memorial shrine with prayer flags, used as a place of meditation. It was built from local stone by Himalayan Monks from Bhutan under the supervision of a Bhutanese lama.

The row of 'Stepping Stones' entices many visitors to stride across the outlet at the west end of the lake to reach the Rock Garden and its plants
– *photos*: **John Hammond**

REFERENCES AND FURTHER READING

Mauchline, Mary. 1974 *Harewood House*
David & Charles Ltd., Newton Abbot, Devon
Lemmon, Kenneth. 1978 *Yorkshire and Humberside, The Gardens of Britain*, No.5. B.T. Batsford, London.
Watson, William. 1928. *Rhododendrons & Azaleas, Present-Day Gardening*. T.C.& L.E.C. Jack, London. 1928.
Lascelles, George. 1995. *The Harewood Rhododendrons*. Unpublished manuscript, 7th Earl of Harewood.
Hammond, John. M. 2009. *The Lost, Forgotten and Abandoned Gardens of Scotland*. RSCG Newsletter, No.3 Winter 2009–10.
Hall, Geoffrey. 1978. *50 Years Gardening at Harewood*. E.P. Publishing Ltd., Wakefield, West Yorkshire.

John M. Hammond *is president of the Scottish Rhododendron Society and a past Director at Large of the American Rhododendron Society. He is active with ARS committees and was awarded an ARS Gold Medal in 2014. He is also a long-standing member of the RCMG.*

Mount Edgcumbe
– notes from a camellia volunteer

Jim Stephens

In 2014, 30 years of nursery work came to an end, leaving me with time on my hands and an accumulation of knowledge that needed an outlet if it wasn't to quickly fade away. I offered my services as a garden volunteer at Mount Edgcumbe in Cornwall, on the condition that I work exclusively on the camellia collection. It was apparent that they were very short staffed and that the camellias, entirely understandably, were not their highest priority.

Since then I have been involved in many aspects of the ongoing management of the collection, including pruning, labelling, record keeping and new planting. The park staff have continued to cut the grass around the collection in late summer and to identify and prune the plants most in need, usually during a couple of weeks in spring. I have helped with the pruning (and occasionally the grass cutting), but usually my time with the collection is spent alone.

I want to describe some of what I have been doing with the collection and to look at some of the issues surrounding its ongoing existence. In terms of the theory and practice of maintaining camellia collections, I see myself as practitioner first, theoretician second. The practical business of looking after plants demands that you think about what you are doing and gives you plenty of time for such reflections.

Mount Edgcumbe hosts the largest of seven National Plant Collections of *Camellia* in the UK. It was started as an International Camellia Society reference collection in 1976, and became a National Plant Collection under

Recently relabelled Camellia 'Firebird' was previously labelled as 'Duchesse Decazes'
– *all photos:* **Jim Stephens**

the NCCPG, now Plant Heritage, in 1980.

Plant Heritage encourages collection holders to put their collection records onto the web-based database system Persephone, which I commenced to do in February 2020. I now have a clearer idea of the scale and scope of the collection, the bare bones of which are: 1,758 records on the system, of which 1,637 are alive and identified, 95 are alive but excluded because they have not been convincingly identified, 24 are dead and two have been withdrawn, taken back off site just weeks after planting to recover from being mauled by deer stags. There are 902 taxa, 887 of which are cultivars.

Getting all the data onto the system has been a big task and the pandemic came at just

Camellia 'Clarrie Fawcett' is another recently relabelled cultivar, which had the earlier label of 'Dreamtime'

Camellia 'Lady MacKinnon' was formerly labelled as 'Lady K'

the right time for doing it, if for very little else. My regular weekly attendance was badly disrupted but at least I had plenty to get on with. Things are now back on a more even keel and I am focusing on the 95 excluded accessions. It is always a great deal easier to determine that a plant is not what the label says it is, but usually much more difficult to be certain enough of its true identity to replace that label. This I am now doing for a considerable number of plants and every time that excluded figure goes down I get a shot of satisfaction that helps me stick to the task.

It would be a wonderful thing to have every plant accurately labelled and it causes me no little angst to know that there are a good few inaccurate labels still on the plants. Taking them off might mean people waste time looking for a label that isn't there and a generic label saying *Camellia japonica* cv. or some such, seems a cop out. I have to admit though, that the chances of identifying the unknowns seem to be diminishing as time goes by.

There are still two batches of plants that

Camellia 'Saturnia' was labelled 'Twiss Cornwall' and now that it has been relabelled, the 'Twiss Cornwall' name will probably sink without a trace

have not been brought within the framework of the National Plant Collection. One is the plants in the Earl's Garden, an area from which the public are excluded unless they have paid to visit the house. There are about 30–40 camellias in it, mostly unlabelled, but I suspect mostly duplicates of cultivars already

93

in the collection. Then there is an altogether different challenge in the Zig Zags.

Lee, the collection curator, told me a few years ago that there were some old camellias in an area about 1km from the main garden, right on the face of the cliff. I visited it, saw some old camellias and didn't see much reason to make my life more complicated. Very recently I found and read a report on the garden by the Garden History Society, in which it says that the area known as the Zig Zags, constructed around 1760, was underplanted with an early 19th-century collection of camellias and other ornamental shrubs. That got my attention. I revisited it and found 19 old camellia plants, ranging from very healthy to nearly dead. I am now trying to find more information on their planting date and contemplating the challenge of identifying them.

Pruning

By far the biggest maintenance task is pruning. It's impossible to know what the people who created the collection had in mind for long-term maintenance. The original plan envisaged planting no closer than 2.5m (8ft) apart, in small groups, which suggests to me that they weren't expecting to prune for perhaps the first two or three decades. What they thought would happen then I don't know but they would surely have been aware that, even at that spacing, the plants would eventually start to crowd each other. They perhaps saw the necessary decisions as being for their successors to make and it is to the credit of Lee Stenning and his staff that they have grasped that particular nettle. The earliest plantings have been in the ground for more than 40 years, the time for doing nothing as a pruning method is long past and decisions have been made about what needs to be done and, with saw and loppers in hand, the team have gone out and done it.

Doing nothing would have resulted in blocks of camellias with leaves and flowers only at the top. It would have been difficult, and unrewarding, to walk through and many varieties would be all but completely hidden. As a collection it would have become deeply unattractive and, in terms of conserving the plants, would also be failing, as inevitably the stronger varieties would smother the weaker ones.

The pruning strategy followed at Mount Edgcumbe has been to 'hat rack' the bushes.

The hat rack method of pruning carried out on 9 April 2019

After three years there is much regrowth but not many flower buds

Plants that are around 3m (10ft) tall are reduced in height and width by around half. Ideally, within a couple of seasons the plants would be back to producing flower buds freely but on a smaller plant. Sometimes that is what happens but mostly it is not. Working within the collection has afforded me the opportunity to observe the response of a wide range of varieties growing in varying conditions to this treatment and to try out some different strategies.

Before looking at pruning in more detail it is worth describing the typical growth pattern of garden camellias. They have a similar growth habit to trees in that the growth is almost entirely at the distal ends of the shoots, the bush getting bigger each season by an amount that is generally quite high to begin with, then slower but steady for many years before tailing off in old age.

Camellias start into growth in spring, between March and May, and make short shoots between 3 and 15cm (1 and 6in) long. Hungry or sickly plants grow very little; vigorous healthy plants, or hard-pruned plants, grow more. Growth then pauses for a few weeks and either the terminal bud develops into a flower bud and the shoot doesn't extend any further or the terminal bud breaks and makes a second increment of growth, usually much longer than the first and up to 60cm (2ft) long and sometimes even more. The second flush may be on every shoot or on very few; if the latter, they are usually at the top of the plant. Some varieties seldom make secondary growth, or cease to do so while still young, others make a lot and carry on doing so for many years. This second flush of growth rarely produces flower buds and can be removed from early autumn, restricting the annual rate of growth to the length of the shorter first flush.

There are big differences between varieties, with some showing very strong apical dominance and only the terminal buds breaking and growing. Where several buds break, it is common for the laterals to develop

flower buds but the terminal bud to break and make a second growth flush. By August or September, the flower buds will be swelling and easily recognised, and all the remaining extension growth can be removed back to the flowering laterals. This shouldn't be done too early or there may be renewed growth, but from late August its removal will:
1) Expose the flower buds on the laterals so they are better displayed when they open in spring.
2) Reduce the total amount of growth made by the bush in the season to the length of the flowering shoots, usually just a few cm.
3) By removing a substantial amount of new leafy growth, possibly reduce the vigour of the bush a little, in favour of flowering, rather than growth, in subsequent years.

In 2018, when we had a very hot dry summer, I saw not a single second flush shoot at Mount Edgcumbe, even on young or recently hard-pruned plants, suggesting that temperature or water stress favours flower bud production and further vegetative growth is curtailed. A hard-pruned (and well nourished) bush of Camellia × williamsii 'Debbie' in my own garden did make secondary growth that year, though less than in the years preceding and following. Suffice it to say that if only one flush of growth is produced or if all secondary growth is removed, the bush will increase in size quite slowly, whereas if there is a lot of secondary growth over a number of years the plant will become very large very quickly.

The pruning advice in the camellia books of my acquaintance is not extensive. The general line is that camellias don't actually *need* pruning, but that they respond well enough if they *are* pruned. It is better to start while the plant is not huge and prune regularly and lightly but, should a plant get much too big, it can be hard-pruned but will then take a couple of years to flower freely again. I think this needs to be more detailed. It is only true to say that they don't need pruning if they are planted where they have enough space to grow

The plant's response to hat rack pruning – strong regrowth confined to a few centimetres below the cut

to maturity without encroaching upon neighbouring plants or where that encroachment is acceptable, as in a group planting. Since that is the exception not the rule in most gardens, there comes a point where pruning *needs* to be a routine part of maintenance. At Mount Edgcumbe, even with plenty of space to begin with, the plants have eventually reached a size where they are crowding each other and pruning is needed.

At Mount Edgcumbe the earlier plantings were made at around 2.5m (8ft) spacing, later plantings at 2m (6½ft) or so. The plants have been allowed to grow unfettered until they are touching each other and it is no longer possible to walk freely between them. At this stage they are usually 2.5–3m (8–10ft) tall. They have then been cut back by about half their height and left to regrow without intervention. Often, by the time the plants get pruned, much of the lower foliage has been shaded out and, when the bushes are pruned,

the subsequent regrowth is heavily concentrated at the ends of the branches and the stems below remain substantially bare. The regrowth is usually prolific and strongly upright, with every cut stem producing between six and ten new shoots.

Pruning is generally carried out in April and May and, by the end of the season, there is typically 20–30cm (8–12in) of new growth. In the following season there will usually be two flushes of growth and 45–60cm (18–24in) for the year is not unusual. The same rate of growth can be repeated for two or three seasons before slowing as flowering recommences.

The upshot is that, in many cases, by the time the plants are back to flowering freely, they are getting close to needing to be pruned again. A minority start flowering within a couple of years but some barely flower at all. When it comes time to prune them again, they cannot be cut at exactly the same place – they must be cut above or below that point. Below is to prune harder than before, through an even thicker stem, so usually they are pruned above, through the cluster of stems from the previous pruning, leading to multiple shoots arising from multiple shoots. The regrowth is denser than before, starting higher than before.

As a method it works insofar as it is better than doing nothing. The plants get space and light and almost always respond by growing strongly, albeit at the expense of losing flowering. Going back to the overall growth pattern of camellias being like trees, this way of pruning is akin to pollarding, though carried out at eight-to-ten-year intervals. At Mount Edgcumbe, with just three full-time gardeners responsible for a huge area, this has generally been done in a spring blitz of a week or two with the help of exchange students and volunteers. It is a simple method, suited for unskilled labour, it is fairly quick and it need not be repeated very often. With limited manpower resources and such a large collection, it is perhaps all that is possible.

In my volunteer capacity I am not able to add greatly to the man hours available for such work. However, I am able to carry out pruning on a low-level, year-round basis. It seems to me that what would be preferable is an approach that lets the plants get to the size required and then keeps them much the same indefinitely. That such a thing is possible is proven by the fact that camellias are used successfully for hedging. In fact, I have only to look out of my window to see two camellias that are maintained as neatly-clipped domes by a local gardening contractor. I am always surprised by how well they flower, though I am not a fan of the approach, favouring a more natural appearance.

In my own garden I have a bush of Camellia japonica 'Bob Hope' that I want to keep at much the size it is now. My garden is small and overcrowded and, as much as I like camellias, I want to grow a lot of other things as well. My approach is twofold. Every year in early autumn I remove any secondary growths with no flower buds on them. The shorter first-flush shoots are between 5 and 10cm (2 and 4in) long so this is as much as the bush increases in size each year. Every two or three years, as flowering finishes, I look long and hard at the bush and imagine it about 30cm (12in) smaller all over. Then I cut the shoots that grow beyond that imaginary outline back to a side shoot within that shape. I aim to keep a natural look as distinct from a clipped outline but reduce the size. I will thin out crowded parts of the bush at the same time to some degree. Again, this is similar to crown reduction in a tree, where the branches are shortened back to a suitably-placed lateral. I try not to concentrate the cuts at the same height, so a natural appearance is achieved. Not only is a neat, clipped appearance something that visually I don't want, but also it means there is a dense layer of leaves over the outside of the bush that shades out any leafy growth within. It is impossible to cut any shoot back more than a few inches without reaching bare wood. An open, irregular bush lets light in so there is nearly always some lower growth to cut back to.

Because I have quite a small garden, I want to maintain the bush below 2m (6½ft) in height, a size that seems to me to be in scale with its surroundings. That height works very well when I am doing my pruning because I can reach the whole bush from the ground with secateurs. I have another plant, Camellia × williamsii 'Charles Colbert', which I have chosen to allow to grow rather bigger, its lower branches removed to create a small tree shape below which I grow shade-loving plants. To prune that I need to use a short step ladder and a telescopic pruner. The pruner is long enough to reach the top but to get to the middle of the top I have to stand back too far, hence the steps.

At Mount Edgcumbe, for the bushes to be in scale with their surroundings, they need to be bigger than my 'Bob Hope'. Given their spacing, a height of 2.5–3m (8–10ft) would

Camellia japonica 'Bob's Tinsie' in April 2019 before and after pruning

Camellia japonica 'Bob's Tinsie' on 16 March 2021 flowering freely (above left) **and on 9 February 2022 it will need pruning again this year** (above right) **with care, three years growth can be removed and still leave the bush quite well furnished**

look best, with a similar width. Almost all parts of the collection are on sloping ground, some very steep, so a step ladder is useless. Pruning can be done with secateurs as high as can be reached, then the telescopic pruner can be used for the rest. Loppers or a pruning saw may come in useful as well. The more that can be done with secateurs the better, because working with the telescopic pruner is much slower. With 1,600 plants in the collection,

the time it takes is an important factor to be considered.

It may be that, on larger plants, this pruning could be carried out every three or four years; there should still be leafy lateral shoots to cut back to. If left any longer the leafy laterals would likely be few. You must know what you're doing with this method. Sawing every branch off at 1.8m (6ft) can be done by untrained staff and done quickly.

Camellia **'Mercury Variegated'**
(bush, above; flower, right)
formerly labelled as 'Masayoshi'

Trimming back to well-placed laterals so as to keep an attractive, natural-looking shape to the bush, and doing so without breaking the tools involved, is more of a challenge.

If the bush is already much too big the question may be whether it can be cut down to a smaller size and then kept small rather than just being allowed to grow up again. I believe the answer is that it can be done but will take a few years to achieve. The plant needs to be cut well below the eventual required height, perhaps 75–90cm (2½–3ft) smaller. The regrowth needs to be thinned and long, whippy shoots removed altogether. I would thin out a third to a half of the regrowth in year one and repeat in year two. By the third season a fairly normal pattern of short first-flush and longer second-flush growth should be emerging and most of the second-flush growth can be removed in late summer or early autumn, hopefully back to laterals bearing flower buds. From then on it needs to be treated as I have described for 'Bob Hope'.

A more measured method of pruning takes much more time to carry out but can be spread across the year, unlike the infrequent heavy pruning, which must be carried out between February and May, generally already a busy time in the garden. It should also be mentioned that pruning at around 90cm (3ft) at Mount Edgcumbe resulted in regrowth at a perfect height for their appreciative deer herd. One or two plants have died after hard pruning, sometimes having made good regrowth in the first year then succumbing as the soft growth became diseased in the winter. A couple of these have started shooting from below ground and should be recoverable. You should never give up on an apparently dead camellia prematurely!

I think what would work best at Mount Edgcumbe is a mix of approaches – some plants left unpruned to develop naturally into small trees, the rest kept at different heights and at different stages in whatever pruning cycle they are in. The measure of success would be that, if it was done well enough, all the plants would look healthy, floriferous, natural and unforced and, the hallmark of good pruning, *no one would notice*.

Virus

Virus infection doesn't seem to be regarded as a major cause for concern among camellia growers and gets dealt with perfunctorily in the books I have seen. Virus infection can cause striking variegation of the blooms and many uninfected varieties have been deliberately infected to that end, the infected plant being given a new cultivar name or getting 'Variegated' tagged onto the existing one. The general view appears to be that the virus responsible is hard to transmit so that infected plants pose no infection risk to other plants growing nearby. I'm not sure that I agree. It's very hard to be sure but I think that in the Mount Edgcumbe collection I am seeing virus variegation appearing in several plants that were hitherto unaffected and that there is also evidence of possibly different virus infection producing different symptoms.

Two plants that have begun to produce variegated flowers are growing quite close to a heavily variegated bush of *Camellia japonica* 'Masayoshi', leading me to wonder if transmission is possible via root contact. Equally they may all have been pruned at the same time without the tools being sterilised between bushes. Other plants that are variegated and shouldn't be are young plants that won't have been pruned. Could they have picked up infection during propagation? It is not a comfortable thought that nurseries may be inadvertently spreading infections through their routine practices, not least because I may have been guilty myself. The progress of the infection through the plant, at least as manifested in variegated flowers, is very slow, so the reputation for it being hard to transmit might be partly attributable to a lack of symptoms for several years after infection occurs.

The other symptoms I've seen are on *Camellia sasanqua* and *Camellia × vernalis* plants where there is some limited yellow mottling of the leaves but a very marked reduction in flower quantity, quality and size. It is possible the two things are not connected but there is one variety where a mottled plant has few flowers and an unmottled plant flowers prolifically. They are however growing in rather different conditions, possibly providing an alternative explanation. It seems to me that this is an under-researched area and that in terms of conserving plants over long periods it potentially poses a serious threat. It seems prudent to treat it as such and to take such steps as are practical to prevent it becoming more of a problem. For my part I shall be carrying something to sterilise my pruning tools in future. It does raise the question of what to do with the virus-infected plants that were planted and labelled as their unvariegated forms.

Extending the collection

In theory there should be two plants of each variety so that there is a back-up should one fail. There are several hundred varieties represented by only one plant, mostly irreplaceable if they are lost. I don't know how you would prioritise which to propagate to create back-ups and, with present resources in space and manpower, planting out another three or four hundred plants to provide duplicates is a fantasy. Even if space and manpower allowed, it could be argued that adding different varieties would be more valuable than duplicating existing ones, even at the risk of losing some altogether.

When a new area was created in 2020, the instincts of both Lee Stenning and myself were to extend the range of the collection rather than plant duplicates of what was already there. The moves by the Rhododendron, Camellia and Magnolia Group to start to compile a much wider register of varieties grown in the UK would help greatly to inform these sorts of decisions. If the basic premise of National Plant Collections is to conserve varieties of garden plants that might

be at risk of being lost without them, then varieties such as *Camellia × williamsii* 'Debbie' and 'Donation' could be safely discarded as being at no risk of being lost in the foreseeable future.

I have been able over my years as a volunteer to plant quite a number of additions to the collection and it is very pleasing to do so. It is always a challenge to get young plants established; it sometimes seems there are more deer inside the deer fence than behind it. The original aims of the collection's founders have been quietly set aside in favour of simply building a diverse collection that stands a reasonable chance of containing material that will still be alive and of interest to future generations, perhaps as far as another 200 years hence. The collection cannot grow much with current resources but at least more have been added than lost in the time I have been involved.

Jim Stephens *is a volunteer at Mount Edgcumbe and formerly worked at the Duchy of Cornwall Nursery with responsibility for Camellias.*

Sustaining deciduous azaleas in a changing climate: lessons learned from the south-eastern United States

Patrick Thompson

Azaleas are well known in the south-eastern United States, but they are so commonplace that they are often overlooked. Horticulturists in the region are mostly familiar with the Asian evergreen cultivars available in the trade. Deciduous azaleas are among those that experts should be sure to become acquainted with if they are going to remain part of the landscape.

This strong, sensitive and striking group of azaleas are widespread but increasingly limited in their range. In the case of the south-eastern US deciduous azaleas, we continue to cultivate the relationship between wild plants and their cultivated versions. Meanwhile, changing temperatures, rainfall and habitat loss pose threats to their survival.

In response, dedicated growers in the area are curating the gene pool in a way that offers solutions for a resilient future in the face of changing climates across the globe. These and other efforts are critical to ensuring the survival of natural and cultivated gene pools in a landscape that is highly developed, managed and populated with intentional plants.

Background

All species of azalea belong to the genus *Rhododendron*, which includes nearly 1,000 species across much of the northern hemisphere and south of the equator in southeast Asia[1]. The taxonomy of the plants in this genus has been in flux since Linnaeus described the now-defunct genus *Azalea* in 1735. Regardless of the lumping or splitting at the level of subgenus, section or species, deciduous azaleas are certainly uncommon. There are fewer than 30 species worldwide, with the majority occurring in the south-eastern US. Southeast Asia is another pocket of deciduous azalea diversity containing at least five different species and subspecies.

A trio of species contributed to the gene pool of the cultivated varieties discussed here. The key species from southeast Asia utilised in Western breeding programmes is *R. molle*. Another deciduous species, *R. occidentale*, is a recruit from its native range in the western US. Lastly, *R. luteum*, Europe's only species of deciduous azalea has a range that spans from southeast Europe into southwest Asia.

As our detailed observations of deciduous azaleas increase, it becomes more apparent that the traditional concept of a species breaks down over and over in these dynamic plants. They do not exist in a simple linear branching phylogenetic tree, and there are easily observed instances of gene flow between species where they co-occur. This ease of gene flow presents challenges to taxonomists but has enabled plant breeders to create the complex hybrids that continue to fascinate gardeners and researchers alike.

DISTRIBUTION OF DECIDUOUS *RHODODENDRON* SPECIES OF INTEREST IN THE SOUTHEASTERN U.S.

A. *Rhododendron alabamense*
B. *Rhododendron austrinum*
C. *Rhododendron cumberlandense*
D. *Rhododendron flammeum*
E. *Rhododendron prunifolium*
★ Donald E. Davis Arboretum
Auburn University
Auburn, Alabama

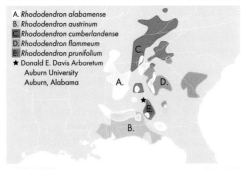

FIG 1: Deciduous azalea species in conservation collections at AU's Davis Arboretum
– Trae Watson

Rhododendron alabamense natural flower form
– *photo*: **Patrick Thompson**

South-eastern US landscape

Deciduous azalea species' ranges overlap throughout most of the southeast US. Sympatric species occupy different habitat niches that preserve in some degree the genetic integrity of a given species. This is evident in Alabama's Bankhead National Forest where *R. canescens* populates the draws and wet weather streams between ridges. The top of the ridges is home to *R. alabamense* and in between you can find intergrades between the two species. In Figure 1, the ranges of a selection of species are shown, but these exist entirely within the range of other widespread species such as *R. canescens* and *R. viscosum*.

Their phenology also acts as an isolating mechanism aiding species preservation – the American azaleas do not bloom all at the same time. In addition, the number of chromosomes a species possesses, or its ploidy level, plays a role. Deciduous azaleas species typically fall into the diploid group with two sets of chromosomes (n=26), or the tetraploid group with four sets of chromosomes (n=52). Even this is not an absolute division of geneflow because there are well-documented examples of triploid individuals occurring that act as bridges

between the two ploidy levels.

Geographic isolation of deciduous azalea species would have been historically limited to pockets at the peripheries. For example, the *R. prinophyllum* populations to the northwest of the region of overlap, and populations of *R. serrulatum* extend into peninsular Florida. In modern times, however, the landscape of the south-eastern US is increasingly developed, logged and crisscrossed with roads. As a result, the remaining pockets of azaleas are isolated, making natural geneflow across populations somewhat obsolete.

European genetic drift

Deciduous azaleas have long been recognised for their beauty. William Bartram described *R. calendulaceum* as "...the most gay and brilliant flowering shrub yet known" in his widely known book *Travels* in 1791. Bartram travelled the range of the American azaleas collecting their banana-shaped seed pods containing hundreds of tiny seeds. The Bartrams were excellent plantsmen, but the taxonomy of their day did not encompass the species now known. William's travels took him through the range of *R. alabamense*, which was not described until 1921, and that of

Unnamed auburn azalea hybrid selected for its superior yellow blotch *R. alabamense* × (*alabamense* × 'Exbury') – *photo*: **Patrick Thompson**

R. colemanii, which was recognised as a species in 2011. His endeavours did play a significant role in seed dispersal as his family's nursery spent decades sending them back to Europe.

Breeding records of centuries past will never align with the names we now have. We do, however, have knowledge of an early 1800s Belgian baker making some of the earliest crosses using the American azaleas. We also know that, not long after, breeders in Ghent and England crossed the American azaleas with *R. luteum* and *R. molle* to further expand the potential of the gene pool. The western azalea, *R. occidentale*, was later added into the mix of these complex hybrids. This all paved the way for the exceptional work that gave us the Knap Hill and Exbury azalea hybrids. Moreover, we know that from the time the first American azaleas crossed the pond, they became subject to various intended and unintended selection pressures.

Seedlings that originated and survived in Europe would have originated only from the azaleas the collectors could access. The physical collection of seeds from an expansive natural population created a significant genetic bottleneck. We are only now learning the proper sampling methods necessary to sufficiently capture a majority of the alleles within a species or genus of plants[2]. The genetic bottleneck set up these azaleas to be predisposed to increased effects of genetic drift, or the loss of certain alleles within a population over generations.

Belgium and England are both more than 15 degrees of latitude north of the epicentre of deciduous azalea diversity in North America. Generations of seedlings grown out at this northern latitude would, with each generation, become increasingly adapted to the more northern climes. As a result, progeny assume no preference for having exceptional heat tolerance. European breeding programmes varied in focal areas for desired traits, but the results by the early 1900s were vigorous plants with a wide palette of colours and large flowers, double flower forms and fragrance, representing hundreds of named varieties that were developed.

Bridging the heat tolerance gap
Key species in these European breeding programmes, such as *R. calendulaceum*, do not do well in the heat and quick-draining soils of areas such as the southern coastal plains of the US. Sites where *R. calendulaceum* could survive in the south-eastern US are in protected microclimates insulated from extreme heat. They thrive in locations like the Blue Ridge Mountains where high elevation acts as a proxy for the security of shady creek banks where they are found at lower elevations. Deciduous azalea heat intolerance is a reality well recognised by gardeners and plant collectors in the US southern coastal plains. The Exbury, Knap Hill, Ghent and Mollis azaleas, among others, can be bought and shipped to this area, but they ultimately die from heat stress during summer when temperatures may reach 40°C for consecutive days, or when rainfall has not occurred in weeks.

A south-eastern US breeding programme, the Auburn Azalea Series, addressing these and other issues, is the culmination of five decades of work by plant collectors, gardeners, plant breeders, retired professors and, for the past decade, the staff of Auburn University's Davis Arboretum in east central Alabama. Years spent in the natural areas of Alabama and Georgia had exposed these collaborators to azaleas that bloomed in spring, summer and fall in shades of white, pink, yellow, orange, red and all their combinations. Efforts to recreate those options in the garden were difficult, and it became clear that even the botanists across the region were challenged when attempting to place appropriate names on the diversity that existed.

Years of collection proved more fruitful than attempting to purchase appropriate plants, though there was a community of azalea enthusiasts in the area that fostered the work. Fred Galle's collection at Callaway Gardens was just an hour down the road. The Dodds, Kelly Strickland, Dr Eugene Aromi, The Beasleys, S.D. Coleman, and many other passionate growers in neighbouring states, helped build the gardens, genetic resources and inspiration that would be the source for the Auburn Azaleas breeding programme.

Retired Auburn University professor R.O. Smitherman initiated the development of a world-class collection of American azaleas at the Davis Arboretum and donated the most successful specimens of more than one thousand hand-pollinated crosses that had taken place over the 1980s and '90s. The breeding programme team focused their efforts on capitalising on the genetics of three late-blooming azaleas that occur nearby: *R. prunifolium*, the fall-blooming form of *R. arborescens* and another vigorous group of azaleas under the name *R. alabamense* 'May Pink' that would eventually be recognised as *R. colemanii*.

These plants were part of an effort to fill gaps in the bloom calendar, but they were also crossed with hybrids such as *R.* 'Gibraltar' and *R.* 'Klondyke' that could not survive here.

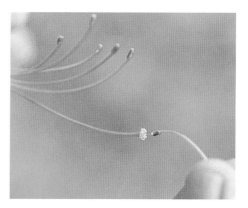

Hand pollination – a simple but effective technique

Auburn Azalea breeder Robert Greenleaf looks over his garden in Auburn, Alabama

Rhododendron flammeum **bred by Greenleaf for its deep red colour** – *photos*: **Patrick Thompson**

Floral diversity in *R. cumberlandense* in Mount Cheaha State Park where it co-occurs with *R. canescens* and *R. arborescens* as well as *R. catawbiense* and *R. minus*

Dwarfed stoloniferous *R. cumberlandense* from Mount Cheaha State Park

Growing in the southern parts of the upper Gulf Coast of the south-eastern US, *R. austrinum* is another species the breeding team relied heavily upon. Here it gets plenty of rain, but is subject to high heat, sandy soils, and even saltwater intrusion. *R. austrinum* is a key species for incorporating heat tolerance into an interspecies breeding programme. As Smitherman systematically crossed the material at hand in as many ways as resources allowed, other Auburn University emeritus colleagues D. Rouse and T. Corley grew out seedlings by the tens of thousands, waiting years to see their blooms, and decades to see how they ultimately performed in Alabama's climate. During this time period, the United States Department of Agriculture acknowledged the increase in average temperatures by shifting the hardiness zone of Auburn from 7b to 8a.

The Auburn Azalea Series breeders also pursued intraspecific breeding programmes. Smitherman searched Alabama and adjacent states for all the nuanced differences in *R. alabamense*. He crossed tall ones with tall ones and short ones with short ones, while incorporating the most fragrant, those with the most distinctive yellow blotch and those with most pleasing pink blush. Corley planted dozens of *R. calendulaceum* on his property to determine which ones persevered in the Alabama heat.

Rouse and Greenleaf sought out and sowed scores of *R. flammeum*. They teased out early bloomers, late bloomers, compact forms, the most exquisite shades of red, even *R. flammeum* flowers that seemed to have a metallic sheen. This proved to be as interesting an exercise as the hybridisation, and an even better fit for the mission of Auburn's Arboretum.

The Arboretum was primarily a teaching garden, home to a collection of native Alabama tree species. Around this same time, a movement was gaining momentum in the public garden community. It was clear that botanical gardens and arboreta were uniquely positioned to be effective agents in efforts to preserve the world's botanical diversity as the threat of an extinction crisis loomed larger. The Global Strategy for Plant Conservation[3] outlined a need for gardens to, among other things, host collections of imperilled plant species to safeguard them from extinction.

The Association of the Public Gardens of America developed its Plant Collections Network to standardise this effort, which is directly connected to Botanic Gardens Conservation International. It is within that framework that the Arboretum welcomed Smitherman's support. The Auburn Azaleas found a home where their aesthetic value could be appreciated and curated under a long-term commitment from the University. The value of the collection as a fundraising tool was not lost on the powers that be. The marketing of the Auburn Azalea Series has bolstered the Arboretum's ability to host a collection of native azaleas that have significant conservation and research value, as well as educational, ecological and aesthetic value.

Addressing threats to survival

The Plant Collections Network prioritises genetic diversity and detailed provenance information in a collection along with detailed labelling, mapping and record keeping. In the quest to achieve their accreditation for developing the world's best collection of *R. alabamense*, Smitherman sought a representative of the species from every state and each county in Alabama where it occurred. Within five years he had gathered representatives from all five states and the majority of counties. However, this task revealed a painful truth. Between his initial collections in the 1970s and '80s, and the Arboretum team's return to the sites around 2010, more than half the sites had been wiped out. Where there were once azaleas, now stood neighbourhoods, strip malls, timber lands and roadsides treated with broad-spectrum herbicides. The genetic bottleneck had begun to tighten on the wild populations.

The problem is not unique to *R. alabamense*. Consider the range of *R. flammeum*, which is a swathe curling from the west side of Georgia across the centre of

the state into South Carolina. In the centre of the state of Georgia is the sprawling metropolis of Atlanta. Deciduous azaleas are good for many things, but repopulating disturbed areas is not one of them. Where *R. alabamense* suffers the death of a thousand cuts, the geneflow of *R. flammeum* has suffered a massive trauma. There is another red azalea in the south, *R. cumberlandense*. It is suffering in Alabama as well, for different reasons. Habitat loss and habitat degradation is a leading cause of extinction, but increasing global temperatures are expected to take an increasing toll in the coming years.

The rate of climate change coupled with the fragmentation of populations is likely to present a real challenge to the survival of many types of deciduous azaleas. Research into these trends and how our azaleas respond is certainly worthwhile for those who find peace of mind knowing that azaleas will be living wild and free for future generations to enjoy. If you want to see *R. cumberlandense* in the heart of its range, the Cumberland Plateau of Tennessee and Kentucky are the place to go. Visitors enjoy the azaleas in Kentucky's Kingdom Come State Park each year.

If plant populations needed to migrate north in order to stay in the climate they need to survive, some species will be able to move better than others[4]. Species that rely on wind or animals for seed dispersal may be able to escape the preserves and parks where they have been protected, but if they do, they will likely land in the designed landscapes that typically don't allow for the slow shift in a species range. In Alabama you find the southernmost occurrences for the Cumberland azalea. It would be a worthwhile research project to conduct experiments comparing the heat tolerances within a species like this. Are the southernmost members of the species the most heat tolerant?

In Alabama, the state's largest remaining population of *R. cumberlandense* occurs in Cheaha State Park, but it is unlikely that this

Rhododendron 'Samford Sorbet' (above) **is a 1987 Smitherman hybrid of *R. colemanii* × 'Gibraltar'**

An unnamed Auburn Azalea hybrid (left) ***R.* (*flammeum × calendulaceum*) × (*atlanticum* × 'Gibraltar')**) **crossed by Smitherman in 1997**
– *photos*: **Patrick Thompson**

population will try to move north to avoid the heat. This population is clinging to increased elevation to raise it above the heat below. This technique can work for a while, but Mount Cheaha is the tallest mountain in the state of Alabama. As the plants move higher up the slope, they are unfortunately on an escalator to extinction. You can't go any higher in Alabama than they already have. If these plants succumb to extreme weather or the increasing threat of wildfires, it could mean the death of the most heat tolerant members of the species. There could come a day when the *R. cumberlandense* in Kingdom Come State Park could be saved by an effort informed by sound science where the assisted migration of the Alabama *R. cumberlandense* gene pool could give both populations a chance to keep moving forward through time.

In most cases once populations are lost in the wild there is no getting them back. The assets required to collect, grow out, repopulate, manage and monitor rare plant populations are in short supply. Alabama is the state with the highest extinction rate in the continental US. The list of species in greater peril than the azaleas is long. The species closest to the brink require that much more effort because the effects of their own genetic bottlenecks are fully present, and many are sliding down the extinction vortex.

A call to action

The good news for deciduous azaleas is that it is not too late. The bottleneck has not become too restricted. There is also much room for the general public's involvement. Once a species is listed under the Endangered Species Act or regulated by CITES, matters become much more complicated. For so many other species in severe decline, conservationists look back and lament the missed opportunities. If only someone had built collections of conservation value before these plants were in dire peril. Auburn's Arboretum is home to some of these collections. The wider the effort to keep well-documented

plant material, the more we can reduce the constriction of the genetic bottleneck. The greater the genetic diversity conserved, the more resilient the remaining gene pool will be.

Efforts to secure a future for deciduous azaleas will require coordination between existing gardens and can help inform foci for new gardens. No one garden or gardener can do enough on their own. This collaborative effort involves building a meta-collection that spans not only across gardens but also continents[5]. Performing gap analyses across gardens show us which species are well represented. Dialling into detailed collections records allows us to see which populations are well represented in cultivation and which need attention. These findings can then inform the work of plant collectors who follow standards set out by groups such as the Center for Plant Conservation to ensure that these collections are not detrimental to the wild populations. Ultimately, maintaining the viability of wild populations is always the best option.

What is the value of preserving the fecundity of the Cumberland azalea, the Oconee or the Alabama azalea? These plants seem to have just begun spreading their evolutionary wings. The radiation of species coming from the south-eastern US has been interrupted by our impacts living on the land. We have also brought these plants into our gardens though. A century of work in Belgium, England and elsewhere produced fantastic plants that could one day depend on a return to their heat-tolerant parents to keep their genes moving forward through time. The escalator to extinction is a short one in a personal garden; many cultivars have already been lost to time. The opportunity before us is to move these living works of art through time. The time to breed new heat-tolerant versions of our favourite deciduous azaleas is now.

Garden clubs and plant societies across the globe are experiencing decreases in membership, and public gardens and arboreta can't address the challenges to deciduous azaleas alone. Perhaps this is a calling to be answered. Perhaps this is the challenge – we need to bring renewed interest to our azaleas. Crowdsourcing this conservation campaign is a promising possibility, as plant collecting in the information age presents a new world of opportunities. Shifting climate patterns and associated extreme weather events present us with the immediate need to answer the call.

The most popular of the Auburn Azaleas, 'War Eagle', is a cross between *R. austrinum* and *R.* 'Gibraltar'. It has striking full trusses of burnt orange flowers that match the colours of the University. It is not too different from 'Gibraltar', except for one key thing. It can be planted in the full sun in south Alabama. In continuing trials that began in 1986, it has proven that, once established, it is extremely resilient.

Even if the variety 'Gibraltar' eventually dies from heat stress in every other garden in the world, perhaps the line will be carried on through 'War Eagle', 'Aubie', 'Tiger', 'Samford Sorbet', 'Patsy's Pink', or 'Plainsman', all progeny of a complex hybrid from Europe and wild azaleas from south Alabama.

Rhododendron **'War Eagle' is a 1985 Smitherman hybrid of *R.* 'Gibraltar' × *austrinum***

Japanese evergreen azalea breeding dates back to before 1500AD. One can hardly imagine what 500 years of breeding could do for the deciduous azaleas. The possibilities are quite exciting. Whether you are working with intraspecies expression, interspecies experiments or introducing wild genes into old blood lines, the last thing a breeder wants to be is limited. To lose any of the American azaleas to extinction or even to see its genetic diversity diminished would be a tragedy. The toolbox represented by the American azaleas has been opened but we have only begun to see the results from utilising it.

There are plants such as *R. colemanii* that grow to small trees up to 7m (23ft) tall, or the 1m (3ft 3in) stoloniferous thickets formed by *R. atlanticum, R. viscosum* and occasionally *R. alabamense.* You can find *R. cumberlandense* and *R. alabamense* pushing through bare rock, while *R. austrinum, R. arborescens* and *R. canescens* tolerate repeated flooding and can grow with their roots right down in the water. Flower colours, size, fragrance and durability, bloom time, salt tolerance, fall colour, foliage variations and heat tolerance are all things waiting to unfurl into our gardens in a plethora of combinations.

Deciduous azaleas make great decorations, but here in Alabama, they are a real part of our ecology that needs to remain intact. There are many ways to play a role in their conservation. Individuals can support public gardens and societies that are working to ensure the plants survive in the natural and the built landscape. Those who are interested in growing American azaleas should consider joining the Azalea Society of America and participating in our seed exchange. Further, maintain good records and find community you can share them with. Lastly, to remain informed on rhododendron conservation efforts worldwide, watch for developments from the Global Consortium for the Conservation of *Rhododendron*, a programme of Botanic Gardens Conservation International led by the Royal Botanic Garden Edinburgh.

Unnamed seedlings of *R.* ('Gibraltar' × *austrinum*) × *austrinum* planted in Samford Park on the campus of Auburn University in East Alabama – *photos:* Patrick Thompson

---

REFERENCES

[1] Galle, F.C. 1985. *Azaleas.* Timber Press, Portland, OR.

[2] Sean Hoban, Taylor Callicrate, John Clark, Susan Deans, Michael Dosmann, Jeremie Fant, Oliver Gailing, Kayri Havens, Andrew L Hipp, Priyanka Kadav, Andrea T Kramer, Matthew Lobdell, Tracy Magellan, Alan W Meerow, Abby Meyer, Margaret Pooler, Vanessa Sanchez, Emma Spence, Patrick Thompson, Raakel Toppila, Seana Walsh, Murphy Westwood, Jordan Wood, M Patrick Griffith Taxonomic similarity does not predict necessary sample size for ex situ conservation: a comparison among five genera. *Proceedings of the Royal Society B*, vol. 287 no. 1926, 2020/5/13

[3] Global Strategy for Plant Conservation. United Nations Convention on Biological Diversity https://www.cbd.int/gspc

[4] Andrew J. Hansen, Ronald P. Neilson, Virginia H. Dale, Curtis H. Flather, Louis R. Iverson, David J. Currie, Sarah Shafer, Rosamonde Cook, Patrick J. Bartlein Global Change in Forests: Responses of Species, Communities, and Biomes: Interactions between climate change and land use are projected to cause large shifts in biodiversity. *BioScience*, Volume 51, Issue 9, September 2001, Pages 765–779

[5] M. Patrick Griffith, Teodoro Clase, Pedro Toribi, Yuley Encarnación Piñeyro, Francisco Jimenez, Xavier Gratacos, Vanessa Sanchez, Alan Meerow, Abby Meyer, Andrea Kramer, Jeremie Fant, Kayri Havens, Tracy M. Magellan, Michael Dosmann, and Sean Hoban. Can a Botanic Garden Metacollection Better Conserve Wild Plant Diversity? A Case Study Comparing Pooled Collections with an Ideal Sampling Model. *International Journal of Plant Sciences* Volume 181, Number 5, June 2020

Patrick Thompson *is Curator of Donald E. Davis Arboretum, Department of Biological Sciences, Auburn University, Auburn, Alabama*

The Centenary Cup Photo Competition 2021

Barry Cooke

Our hopes of holding an in-person Centenary Cup competition alongside the Group AGM were once again dashed by Coronavirus restrictions. We had to hold a virtual AGM by Zoom and the Centenary Cup became a photographic competition for the second year running. It's not the same as an in-person competition where we can see real entries and enjoy each other's company but there was nothing else for it.

Each photograph entered in the competition was given a unique entry number to maintain the anonymity of the entrant. This made it easier for the panel of judges to identify their selections. The number appears after the plant name and all entries are shown on the Group website, where the photos can be enlarged. The competition comprised seven classes:

1. Rhododendron species – 131 entries
2. Rhododendron hardy hybrids – 177 entries
3. Tender Rhododendrons, including Vireyas – 34 entries
4. Deciduous azaleas – 47 entries
5. Evergreen azaleas – 45 entries
6. Camellia – 118 entries
7. Magnolia – 50 entries

Initially each judge selected the best three photos from their allocated class and the first-place photographs in the seven classes were then judged against each other by the whole panel of judges. None of the judges entered the competition. In all, 33 Group members entered the competition sending in more than 600 photographs. The first, second and third place entries in each class are shown on the pages that follow.

The winning photograph was *R.* 'Fortune' sent in by Roderick and Mary White. They were presented with the Centenary Cup in late August by Vice Chairman Barry Cooke.

I must thank Pam Hayward for acting as the steward of the competition, a very time-consuming role; also, thanks to the seven Group members who judged the competition and gave their time so freely.

I sincerely hope that we will be able to have an in-person Centenary Cup competition at Ramster Garden in May 2022.

Mary and Roderick White with the Centenary Cup in August 2021 for their photo of *Rhododendron* 'Fortune' – *photo:* **Polly Cooke**

Class 1: hardy species rhododendron, truss or spray

FIRST *Rhododendron keysii* 0159
photo: **Alan Pedrick**

SECOND *R. praestans* 0081 *photo*: **Mark Bobin**

THIRD *R. multiflorum* var. *purpureum* 0582
(formerly *menziesia*) *photo*: **Pam Hayward**

Class 2: hardy hybrid rhododendron, truss or spray

FIRST & CENTENARY CUP COMPETITION WINNER
R. 'Fortune' 0245 *photo*: **Roderick & Mary White**

SECOND *R.* 'Sappho' 0196 *photo*: **Mark Bobin**

THIRD *R.* 'Loderi Sir Joseph Hooker' 0315
photo: **Philip Eastell**

Class 3: tender species or hybrid rhododendron, inc Vireyas, truss or spray

FIRST *R.* 'Cara Mia' (Vireya) 0146
photo: **Andy & Jenny Fly**

SECOND *R. loranthiflorum* (Vireya) 0392
photo: **Andy & Jenny Fly**

THIRD *R.* 'Robert Bates' (Vireya) 0240
photo: **Andy & Jenny Fly**

Class 4: deciduous azalea, truss or spray

FIRST *R.* 'Bartholo Lazzari' 0168
photo: **Andy & Jenny Fly**

SECOND *R.* 'Gibraltar' AGM 0346
photo: **Fiona Campbell**

THIRD *R. schlippenbachii* 0084 *photo*: **Mark Bobin**

Class 5: evergreen azalea, truss or spray

FIRST *R.* 'Aya kammuri' Wilson No19 0265
photo: **Polly Cooke**

SECOND *R.* 'George Hyde' 0270 *photo*: **Polly Cooke**

THIRD *R.* 'Saotome' Wilson No21 0293
photo: **Polly Cooke**

Class 6: camellia species or hybrid bloom or spray

FIRST *C.* 'Freedom Bell' 0232 *photo*: **Russell Beeson**

SECOND *C. forrestii* 0068 *photo*: **Glynne Jones**

THIRD *C. japonica* 'Adelina Patti' AGM 0442
photo: **Jim Stephens**

Class 7: magnolia species or hybrid, bloom or spray

FIRST *Magnolia sprengeri* 0317
photo: **Philip Eastell**

SECOND *M.* **'White Caviar'** 0363
photo: **John Marston**

THIRD *M. tengchongensis* 0364
photo: **Roger Clark**

RHS Awards 2021

The Rhododendron, Camellia and Magnolia Group Committee has the privilege of recommending individuals for four prestigious RHS annual awards and a fifth award for an exhibit shown to the RHS in that year. The process of nomination and voting takes place in the autumn and the winning candidates for the 2021 awards have been ratified by the Woody Plant Committee.

THE A J WALEY MEDAL AWARDED TO PADDY MACKIE

This medal was instituted in 1937, by the late Alfred J. Waley, to provide an annual award to a working gardener involved in the cultivation of rhododendrons. The fund was transferred from the Rhododendron Association to the RHS in 1946. Since 2013 the scope of this award has been extended to include any individual who is involved in the practical cultivation of rhododendrons.

Paddy Mackie, the 2021 A. J. Waley Medal recipient, is one of Britain and Ireland's leading plantsmen and has been a passionate grower and advocate of rhododendrons throughout his long and interesting life. Born into a family of famous Ulster gardeners, Paddy began to create his present garden in 1959, then aged 28. The prospect was daunting; a windswept, drowned drumlin in Strangford Lough, with just a single mature ash tree.

More than 60 years on, visitors to Mahee Island have little idea of the site's challenging origins. Given the benign climate of this coastal area, the garden looks much older, with giant towering eucalypts, eucryphias, magnolias, camellias, schimas and lush tree ferns. Rhododendrons reign supreme in this garden however, all choice species and the best of the old and new hybrids, deliberately selected to benefit from the sheltered coastal microclimate.

The rhododendron collection at Mahee is one of the finest private collections on the

Paddy Mackie with his *Rhododendron sinogrande* at Mahee Island – *photo:* **Tracy Hamilton**

island of Ireland, cultivating most of the newly-introduced species such as *Rhododendron kesangiae*. Paddy Mackie has been a major exponent for the popularisation and cultivation of rhododendrons, not just in Northern Ireland, but right across the island of Ireland, and has long promoted these emperors of the plant world.

THE LODER RHODODENDRON CUP AWARDED TO SEAMUS O'BRIEN

Presented in 1921 by the late Gerald Loder (Lord Wakehurst) in memory of his brother Sir Edmund Loder Bt. This award recognises the value of the work of the recipient to horticulture.

Seamus O'Brien is awarded the Loder Rhododendron Cup for 2021. He has been Head Gardener at Kilmacurragh, once the home of the Acton family, since 2006 and has transformed the gardens and trebled its visitor numbers in this time. Seamus has helped to save as many historic rhododendrons and conifers as possible from within these gardens that were planted in the late 18th and early 19th centuries, and conserve native Irish hedgerow plants and wildflowers. He has added an eclectic range of endangered genera from around the world, including many that he collected himself from countries as diverse as Sikkim, China, Chile, South Africa and Tasmania.

Not only has Seamus transformed the gardens at Kilmacurragh, but also his plant knowledge and stories about plants and people is superb. He generously shares this information through his enthralling talks and highly-acclaimed books, including *In the footsteps of Augustine Henry* (2011) and *In the footsteps of Joseph Dalton Hooker* (2018). He launched his book about Hooker to the RCMG at Exbury in 2019, and his recent online

Seamus O'Brien on one of Joseph Hooker's 1849 *Rhododendron arboreum* collections from Sikkim at the NBG Kilmacurragh – *photo*: **Richard Johnston**

presentation featuring the rhododendrons of Sikkim, were both highly praised by those who attended. Seamus is Irish Branch Chair of the RCMG and has actively re-established our Group in Ireland for the past couple of years.

THE DAVID TREHANE CAMELLIA CUP AWARDED TO EVERARD DANIEL

Presented to the RHS in 2000 by Jennifer Trehane in memory of her father, David Trehane, the Cup is awarded annually to a person who has significantly promoted or increased knowledge on camellias.

Everard Daniel is the 2021 David Trehane Camellia Cup recipient. He is quite simply a walking encyclopaedia of plants. Everard is well known to many of us in the southern branches of the Group for his extensive knowledge of trees and shrubs, notably rhododendron hybrids, magnolia and hydrangea. His knowledge and expertise with camellia is no exception. He grows a variety of rare and unusual camellias for his own pleasure and supplements these with innumerable garden visits to see and broaden his knowledge of the genus. He has a keen eye for detail, which is invaluable for naming. He willingly shares his knowledge of camellia and is always able to give sound cultivational advice. Everard is a truly knowledgeable

Everard Daniel – *photo:* **Sarah Hardman**

currently six new varieties under trial. Mark is inherently patient and ruthlessly discerning, releasing varieties only when content with their performance and ease of propagation. There are no B-graders in the Jury catalogue. Among these are a 'best red' contender to upgrade 'Vulcan'; a more garden-friendly, longer-flowering 'Lanarth'; new 'Fairys' including a truly compact variety and a colour breakthrough flowering in shades of purple to deep pink with dark foliage.

Exciting work in progress may soon realise Mark's dream of a large yellow deciduous bloom with cup-and-saucer form.

Our gardens are all the richer for Mark's dedication, discernment and creativity.

ambassador for camellias who readily shares and therefore spreads his knowledge and enthusiasm within the Group and far beyond.

THE JIM GARDINER MAGNOLIA CUP AWARDED TO MARK JURY

The cup was awarded for the first time in 2017, in honour of magnolia enthusiast and Vice President of the RHS, Jim Gardiner. It is awarded annually to a person who has significantly promoted or increased the knowledge of the genus Magnolia.

Mark Jury, who receives the Jim Gardiner Magnolia Cup for 2021, is highly respected internationally in the magnolia world. Few gardens with a collection of magnolias will be missing a Jury creation. Mark has followed in his father Felix's footsteps to build on the legacy of iconic varieties such as 'Iolanthe' and 'Apollo'. Through his inherited eye and learned skills he has sustained, matched and even topped that legacy with classics such as 'Felix Jury', 'Black Tulip' and 'Honey Tulip'. Moreover, he has ventured into hybridising the former *Michelia* species, producing ground-breaking varieties for all gardens in the now widely available Fairy magnolia series.

His imagination has not stilled; there are

Mark Jury with some of his seedling Magnolia flowers – *photo:* **Abbie Jury**

THE ROTHSCHILD CHALLENGE CUP

Not awarded in 2021.

Appreciation

Harold Greer and *Rhododendron* **'Chipper' at Greer Gardens Nursery in 2018 –** *photo:* **Brenner Wiegard**

HAROLD ELDON GREER 1945–2021

An extraordinary career spanning more than six decades ended unexpectedly with Harold Greer's passing this past August. Though it came far too soon, Harold left us while occupied as he likely would have chosen – in the display garden he created for The Springs at Greer Gardens, a senior retirement facility. The high-end retirement home and garden, featuring many of Harold's favourite rhododendrons, is located on the 14-acre property of Greer's retail plant nursery, widely known as 'Famous for the Rare and Unusual'.

The Greer connection to ornamental gardening began in the early 1950s when Harold was a pre-adolescent. His father Edgar Greer was an insurance salesman who enjoyed growing plants as a hobby. Recently moved from California and looking forward to retirement, he wanted to expand that interest

and perhaps operate a small hobby nursery. With that in mind, a vacant lot was purchased next to the family home in the River Road area near Eugene, Oregon. During this time, Harold began helping in the family garden and soon demonstrated a precocious interest in ornamental plants. He often accompanied his father on plant-hunting expeditions, absorbing even more from growers they visited. Edgar Greer was at first mostly interested in roses and knew nothing of rhododendrons. That was to change, however, when he became acquainted with Joe Steinmetz.

Steinmetz was growing rhododendrons from the James Barto collection. Barto was a pioneer grower of that plant genus on the High Pass Road near Junction City in Oregon prior to the 1940s. With Edgar Greer's purchase of about 100 of those plants from Steinmetz the stage was set for an extraordinary career path.

By the late 1950s all the available land at their River Road home was filled with plants and a search began for more land. In late 1961 they purchased just over three acres from a nurseryman on Good Pasture Island Road, at the time on the western outskirts of Eugene, later adding an adjoining 11 acres. Harold became known as a rhododendron enthusiast and as grower, hybridiser, plant collector, author, photographer, nurseryman, speaker and all-round ornamental garden promoter.

A garden visit with Harold was a truly 'eye-opening' experience as he pointed out details one might otherwise miss in a plant's bark, leaf features, flower colour or shape and so on. His capacity to note small details others often overlooked, coupled with an extraordinary memory, allowed him to identify specific cultivars with unfailing accuracy. In particular, Harold's ability to identify hundreds of hybrid rhododendrons – often with only a glance – was widely recognised and legendary among enthusiasts of the genus.

Images from Harold's thousands of photographs taken over the years have been widely published with both his writing and others, including a stunning portrait of a rhododendron flower bud at the threshold of opening as the cover image for the highly regarded periodical *Smithsonian*. He authored three editions of *Greer's Guidebook to Rhododendrons* and co-authored, with Homer Salley, *Rhododendron Hybrids*, First and Second Editions. Both provided detailed information on hybrid rhododendron parentage and were based on records the Greers began keeping as a means of supporting their annual hybridising programme, amounting to 80–100 crosses in some years, while still in their River Road home. In his lifetime, Harold raised, named, introduced, registered and distributed an amazing 52 crosses; in addition to thousands and thousands of rejected seedlings.

Even the descriptions of ornamental plants and trees in the illustrated annual catalogue for 'Greer Gardens', which typically ran to 150 pages in close-typed small font, was an extraordinary soft-backed book that had passed its 40th year of publication and became a valued reference work for many. For example: "*Magnolia* 'Wada's Memory' – (-10°F, USDA Zones 6-8) in March and April this young, precocious bloomer yields drooping 7in white blooms that are deliciously fragrant. Blooms at age 10. New leaves emerge red, becoming green as they mature. A vigorous grower, it grows narrowly upright to 20-25', achieving a pyramidal shape. Prefers sun with partial shade. Named for the esteemed nurseryman K. Wada of Japan."

Somehow, Harold found time to be active in the American Rhododendron Society (ARS) for most of his life, serving at District and Board level in many roles and was President from 1987–89. He is one of the few members to receive all three medals from the ARS: Bronze, Silver and Gold, the last as long ago as 1989. Harold has organised many of the highly successful West Coast ARS Conventions across the years, regularly giving stunning presentations of his own photography using multi-projection equipment. He has also organised and led overseas tours for ARS members to many rhododendron destinations, assisted by his wife Nancy.

Harold's many friends in the rhododendron world will have good reason to be thankful to him for his kindness, encouragement, and for generously supporting them with plant material, or with photographs to use in their presentations and publications.

John M Hammond *is President of the Scottish Rhododendron Society and a past Director at Large of the American Rhododendron Society. He is active with ARS committees and was awarded an ARS Gold Medal in 2014. He is also a long-standing member of the RCMG.*

Gordon K Wylie *is a past President of the American Rhododendron Society and remains active with committees and as a Board Advisor. He was awarded an ARS Gold Medal in 2001.*

Notes from the International Rhododendron Registrar 2021

SHARON MCDONALD

2021 saw 80 registrations, from 29 registrants, originating from eleven countries. This year the registrations were as follows: 38 from the USA, twelve from Australia, six from France, five each from Latvia and New Zealand, four each from Poland and the UK, three from Japan and one each from Belgium, China and Finland.

There were 37 elepidotes, 16 lepidotes (15 of which were vireyas), 21 evergreen azaleas and six deciduous azaleas.

This year, 20 different species appeared in parentages. *R. kochii* Stein, first published in *Gartenflora* 27: 193 (1885) has not been listed as a parent before. It is a vireya, native to the Philippines, found growing up to 2,300m. The flowers, 10+/truss, are small, narrowly funnel-shaped and white. The leaves are small and elliptical. It grows to around 10m in height. Andrew Rouse (Australia) has crossed *R. kochii* with *R. macgregoriae* F. Muell., to create 'Simon Begg' (named for a past-President of the Australian Rhododendron Society). *R. macgregoriae* is also a vireya, native to New Guinea, found growing up to 3,350m. The flowers, up to 15/truss, are small, shortly tubular funnel-shaped and can be variable in colour, with yellow, orange, red and pink forms, some also having orange or yellow throats. The leaves are elliptical to ovate and larger than those of *R. kochii*. It grows to around 5m in height.

'Simon Begg' has small, tubular campanulate flowers, up to 20/truss, which are white, with a light purplish pink blush at the margins. The leaves, which are elliptic, fall between that of the two parents size wise. It has grown to 2m × 1m in 15 years. It was one

Rhododendron 'Simon Begg'
– *photo:* **Andrew Rouse**

of 15 vireya registrations this year, twelve from Australia and three from New Zealand.

Ten of the 12 vireyas from Australia this year came from Neil Puddey. All were bright and exotic looking, but 'Saint-Leu Sunset' ('Dorothy' × 'Beejay Bay') is my favourite. It has tubular funnel-shaped flowers, the tube is a bright yellow, the lobes are bright red and you can see why it has sunset in its name! The leaves are glossy above, with brown scales below and it has grown 1 × 0.5m in six years. Saint-Leu is a small town, with a famous surfing beach, on Réunion Island (in the Indian Ocean).

Rhododendron **'Saint-Leu Sunset'** – *photo:* **Neil Puddey**

The three vireyas from New Zealand all came from Browns Nursery. 'Dainty Belle' and 'Simply Red' both have neat little red flowers, but 'Elouise' ('Silver Thimbles' open pollinated) has small, understated flowers, with barely overlapping lobes, that are white, with a pink blush around the margins at maturity. The small leaves are glossy, opening with scattered light green indumentum becoming mid to dark green upon maturity. It has grown to 0.5 × 0.5m in nine years.

Moving on from the vireyas, 'Teuvo' (*R. brachycarpum* ssp. *brachycarpum* Tigerstedtii Group × *R. microgynum*) from Kristian Theqvist (Finland) has slightly untidy, but glowing, purplish red flowers, with scattered spots and stripes of a slightly darker tone on the dorsal and adjacent lobes. The large leaves have decurved margins and the undersides are covered in thick yellow brown hairs. It has grown to 1 × 1m in ten years. 'Teuvo' is named for Kristian's 94-year-old father.

Rhododendron 'Elouise' – *photo:* **Pauline Brown**

Rhododendron 'Teuvo' – *photo:* **Kristian Theqvist**

Rhododendron 'Bouboule' – *photo:* **Marc Colombel**

Rhododendron 'Noto-akari' – *photo:* **Yoko Otsuki**

'Bouboule' ('Horizon Monarch' × 'L'Engin') is from Marc Colombel (France) and the ball-shape of the truss and beautifully frilled, colourful lobes made me smile as soon as I saw it. The pale pink and yellow blends of the lobes contrast well with the yellowish-pink margins and splashes of red at the base of the throat and in the sparse spotting along the basal margins of the dorsal lobe. Bouboule was the nickname of Marc's French Bulldog.

The three registrations from Japan were all Noto-Kirishima cultivars. Kirishima azaleas (Kirishima-tsutsuji), originate from around Mount Kirishima on the island of Kyushu in Japan. They are hybrids of *R. kiusianum* × *R. kaempferi* or further, subsequent hybrids. This cross is known as *R.* × *obtusum* by some or Obtusum Group by others. Some of these azaleas were introduced to Edo (now Tokyo) in the 17th century and became known as Edo-Kirishima azaleas. These azaleas were introduced to the Noto peninsula, where they mutated in the harsher conditions and are now considered distinct from the original Kirishima azaleas and are given the name Noto-Kirishima azaleas.

The three registrations were all submitted by the Noto-Kirishima-Tsutsuji no Sato (a not-for-profit organisation) formed, in 2004, by volunteers who are engaged in the

protection, conservation, research and information dissemination of and about these azaleas. The three cultivars are all chance seedlings found in a garden in Noto and are all small, evergreen azaleas.

'Noto-akari' (meaning Noto lights) has funnel-shaped, hose-in-hose red flowers, with a few, scattered slightly darker spots on the dorsal and adjacent lobes. The small leaves are matt and covered in transparent, colourless hairs. It has grown to 2 × 2m in 30 years. The cultivar has a brighter colour in the UK than Japan. It blooms from mid-April to the end of May, with the calyx often persisting into July.

'Noto-no-asahi' (meaning sunrise of Noto) has single, funnel-shaped red flowers, quite heavily marked with darker toned spots on the dorsal and adjacent lobes. Its leaves are matt,

R. 'Noto-no-asahi' – *photo:* **Yoko Otsuki**

R. 'Noto-no-yūhi' – *photo:* **Yoko Otsuki**

R. 'Elizabeth Cosby' – *photo:* **Caroline Beck**

and covered with short, silky, greenish-white hairs. It has grown to 1.65 × 1.65m in 20 years.

'Noto-no-yūhi' (meaning sunset of Noto) has single, funnel-shaped red flowers, with some darker toned spots on the dorsal and adjacent lobes, but the calyx is one-third the length of the corolla, giving a semi-double effect. The leaves are matt, with scattered, short and silky, dull white hairs. It has grown to 1 × 0.9m in ten years.

All three cultivars are hardy to -20°C, with 'Noto-no-asahi' and 'Noto-no-yūhi' becoming semi-evergreen, with the remaining leaves turning bronze red.

Robert Stewart (USA) sent the most registrations (17) from one person this year. All his cultivars are evergreen azaleas and many are double or semi-double. They are all named for people, including three members of the Cosby family, who started a garden in Virginia, USA in 1980. The garden has grown over the years and now runs to around 80 acres. The Cosbys have planted close to 2,000 different azalea hybrids and around 300 different rhododendrons. In 2014, the Lewis Ginter Botanical Garden agreed to manage the garden and it is now named the Lewis Ginter Nature Reserve. The Cosby's continue to live on the Reserve and work with the Botanic Garden staff to ensure that the Reserve continues to run smoothly.

'Elizabeth Cosby' is single-flowered, with rounded, overlapping lobes. It is white, with deep pink margins and is heavily spotted with red on the dorsal lobe and lightly spotted on the adjoining edges of the adjacent lobes. It has white filaments, with dark anthers and the style is bright pink, with a reddish stigma. Its leaves are mid-green and semi-glossy. It has grown to around 0.8 × 1m in ten years.

'Lynwood Cosby' is a beautiful, full double with up to 29 lightly frilled, red lobes per flower. The sexual parts are largely absent, with just a few stamens present. The leaves are mid-green and semi-glossy. It has grown to around 0.6 × 0.6m in ten years.

R. 'Lynwood Cosby' – *photo:* **Caroline Beck**

R. 'Monsignor Roy Cosby' – *photo:* **Caroline Beck**

R. 'Bengt's Foxy Lady' –
photo: **Gospodarstwo Szkółkarskie Ciepłucha**

'Monsignor Roy Cosby' is single-flowered, with five to six white lobes, which are striped and speckled with red and which has yellow-green spotting on the dorsal lobe and on the margins of the adjacent lobes. The stamens may occasionally be petaloid, otherwise they are greenish, with brownish white and red anthers and the style is greenish white with a green stigma. The leaves are olive green and matt. It has grown to 0.6 × 0.6m in ten years.

Gospodarstwo Szkółkarskie Ciepłucha (Poland) registered four rhododendrons originating from Bengt Carlsson (Sweden). All four are hybrids of *R. yakushimanum* and share its heavily tomentose leaves. They are named for the hybridiser and for animals with thick, woolly coats ('Bengt's Bear', 'Bengt's Foxy Lady', 'Bengt's Lynx' and 'Little Bear').

'Bengt's Foxy Lady' (*R. yakushimanum* hybrid) has funnel-shaped, pink flowers and the leaves are broadly lanceolate. When young the indumentum is an intense silver colour and covers the entire leaf, but at maturity the indumentum on the upper surface has mostly disappeared and become cream underneath. It has grown to around 1 × 1m in ten years.

The Rhododendron Nursery Babīte, University of Latvia, sent five registrations this year. Of the five I was most taken with 'Miuaniz' ('Homebush' × 'Austra'), which has wonderful, strongly domed trusses packed full of lovely pink, slightly reflexed, hose-in-hose, flowers, with touches of a yellowish tone deep in the throat. There are no visible stamens, but it has a red-purple style, with a green stigma. The leaves are elliptic and matt and it has grown to 2.4 × 2.4m in 21 years.

Last, but not least, is probably my favourite of this year's registrations, 'Brewster Firecracker' (parentage unknown). Originating from Robert Furman (USA), it was registered by his daughter, Karen Humphries (USA). It has broadly funnel-shaped flowers, with glorious, creamy, slightly ruffled, lobes, with nearly symmetrical spotted flares of red at the base of each lobe. The filaments are whitish, with brownish red anthers and the style is greenish yellow, with a red stigma. The ovary is also red. The leaves are oblanceolate, olive green, glossy, and very slightly mucronate. It has grown to 1.2 × 0.9m in 20 years.

R. 'Miuaniz' – *photo*: **Rhododendron Nursery Babite**

These are all personal choices and I have only highlighted a few of the many lovely and interesting plants included in this year's registrations.

Moving to administration, the RHS Registrars have started working with their IT colleagues to look at the best database platform to move the Registers to. We are at the very start of the process, reviewing the current database, looking at how it works for us and other users and where we can make changes/additions. We are passing this information on to IT, so that they can choose the best product for us to migrate to and, hopefully, get online. I hope to have much more on this in the next 'Notes'.

Finally, just to say, do please get in touch with me, with any queries, additions or corrections, as well as with registrations. My email address is: sharonmcdonald@rhs.org.uk and post should be sent to The International Rhododendron Registrar, RHS Garden Wisley, Woking, Surrey GU23 6QB, UK.

R. 'Brewster Firecracker'
– *photo*: **Donna Delano**

Notes from the International Magnolia Registrar 2021

MATTHEW LOBDELL

Magnolia Society International has been recording information on *Magnolia* cultivars since the 1960s. Early issues of the *Newsletter of the American Magnolia Society* (the predecessor of the journal *Magnolia*) often included requests for lists of or descriptions of cultivars known to members. Responses, as well as literature research, were used to build an extensive card catalogue that was eventually compiled and published by Jack Fogg and Joe McDaniel as *The Checklist of Cultivated Magnolias* in 1975. In 1994, Larry Langford completed an extensive update, publishing a revised and expanded edition.

Towards the end of 2021, efforts by The Morton Arboretum and Magnolia Society International allowed for the publication of the third edition of the cultivar checklist. It is available in the peer-reviewed open-access journal *HortScience*, available to all free of charge. More than 2,000 cultivar epithets were researched during the project, making it the most comprehensive listing of *Magnolia* cultivars to date. I hope it is similarly useful to today's magnolia enthusiasts and encourage any information on new or otherwise unlisted introductions.

Of course, magnolia introduction is still active, and there are already three cultivars not reflected in the most recent checklist!

Lawrence Banks (Kington, Herefordshire, England) registered two crosses of 'Anne Rosse' × 'Purple Breeze', named 'Lucy' and 'Esther' after his granddaughters. The former measures 7.5m (25ft) high with an upright habit and bright pink flowers, while the latter is slightly shorter to 5m (16ft) in height, with a broader canopy and pinkish-purple flowers.

Magnolia 'Lucy'

Magnolia 'Esther' – *photos:* Lawrence Banks

Erland Ejder (Laholm, Sweden), Kang Yongxiang (Yangling, Shaanxi, China) and Wang Yaling (Xi'an, Shaanxi, China) registered *Magnolia sprengeri* var. *sprengeri* 'Cliffhanger', a cultivar selected from a spontaneous tree in Red Valley, Shaanxi, China, and, owing its name to the precarious growing position on a narrow ledge several metres above the valley floor. Originating from the northernmost area of the species distribution, it is expected to be one of the winter hardiest *M. sprengeri*, already demonstrating hardiness to -15°c (5°F).

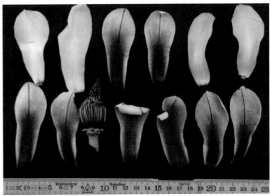

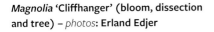

Magnolia 'Cliffhanger' (bloom, dissection and tree) – *photos*: **Erland Edjer**

Additionally, it is the first cultivar of *M. sprengeri* var. *sprengeri*, as opposed to the more southern and horticulturally prominent *M. sprengeri* var. *diva*, to be formally registered.

More details on the above selections are available in Issue #108 of *Magnolia*. New cultivar registrations are processed on a rolling basis and published in this biannual journal, available to all members of Magnolia Society International.

REFERENCES

Fogg, J. M., Jr. and J. C. McDaniel (eds) (1975) *Checklist of the cultivated Magnolias.* vii +54pp. +12pp. American Horticultural Society Plant Sciences Data Center, Mt. Vernon, VA.

Langford, L.W. (1994) *Checklist of the cultivated Magnolias*, rev. ed. 100pp. Magnolia Society.

Lobdell, M.S. (2021) Register of Magnolia Cultivars. *HortScience* 56(12):1614–1675. doi: https://doi.org/10.21273/HORTSCI16054-21

Matthew Lobdell *is Head of Collections and Curator of The Morton Arboretum, Lisle, Illinois, USA*

European Camellia Registrations 2021

REPRINTED COURTESY OF THE INTERNATIONAL CAMELLIA SOCIETY AND THE INTERNATIONAL CAMELLIA REGISTER

camellia enthusiast. Introduced by Savioli F.lli. azienda Florovivaistica Nursery in Verbania Pallanza, Italy. The plant is bushy and open, growing at a medium rate. The cultivar has round, green flower buds. These open over a long mid-season period as single Higo-type blooms, with white base colour and crimson streaks ranging from narrow to broad, like some of the "brocade" Higo camellias. Yellow stamens are in a ume-jin higo arrangement; filaments are white. Flowers are similar to 'Yamato-nishiki' but with a smaller centre relative to the size of the flower W9–10cm. Spent blooms fall whole. Flat leaves are lustrous dark green on both sides, averaging L9cm and W6cm.

- **C. 'Chouchou'**
(*C. japonica*) Reg. No. 155. Seedling of 1993 of unknown parentage, first blooming in 1998. Originated by Joséphine Béréhouc, of Quimper, Brittany, France, who named the cultivar, with the endearment equivalent to "little darling". Introduced by Pépinières de Kervilou (Béréhouc), of Quimper. It has been regularly shown in the floral exhibitions of Breton camellia associations. The floriferous plant is of bushy, dense growth, with a medium growth rate. Buds oval and green. The informal double blooms feature wavy outer petals, while at the heart, small stamens are mixed with petaloids and erect petals. The bloom is a white faintly blushed pink, of medium-sized H4cm W12cm. Leaves are medium-sized, light green, oval and short acuminate. Mid-season blooming.

- **C. 'Dr. Hubert Linthe'**
(*C. japonica* Higo-type) Reg. No. 156. Seedling of *C. japonica* Higo 'Ōkan' and unknown pollen parent. Originated in 2007 by camellia nurseryman Peter Fischer, of Wingst, Germany; first flowered in 2015. Named by Higo camellia specialist Dr. Georg Ziemes, of Düsseldorf, Germany, in honour of German physician Dr. Hubert Linthe, a long-standing member of the ICS and passionate

- **C. 'Eng. Jorge Garrido'**
(*C. reticulata*) Reg. No. 157. *C. reticulata* seedling of unknown parentage. First bloomed in 2013 by António Assunção, camellia specialist in Guimarães, Portugal, and named by him in honour of Eng. Garrido, a Portuguese engineer. The cultivar is a slow-growing, dense and prostrate plant. Elongated, red flower buds open very late in the season into imbricated formal double blooms. Medium-sized

blooms have yellow stamens and white filaments.
Dark green, glossy and acuminate leaves average
L11cm long and W5cm. Spent flowers shatter.

- C. 'Evangeline Palo'
(*C. japonica*) Reg. No. 158. Seedling of *C. japonica*
Higo 'Shin-ōta-haku' and unknown pollen parent.
Seedling originated in 2013 by Dr. Georg Ziemes, of
Düsseldorf, Germany; it first bloomed in 2018. It is
named in honour of a friend and gardening
colleague of Dr. Ziemes, who describes Mrs. Palo as
a woman with "two green thumbs". Introduced by
Savioli F.IIi. azienda Florovivaistica Nursery in
Verbania Pallanza, Italy. The plant is upright, with
rapid growth. The round-oval flower buds are green
with a white tip and open from early to late season,
with moderate flower production. The flowers are a
rose-form double, white (RHS Colour Chart: White
Group 155 C-D), and W11–12cm. Spent flowers fall
whole. Leaves are flat, with upper side dark green
and under side slightly lighter green, of an average
L9cm and W7.5cm.

- C. 'Lineostic'
(*C. japonica*) Reg. No. 159. *C. japonica* seedling of
unknown parentage. Originated in 2005 by
Joséphine Béréhouc, of Quimper, Brittany, France;
first bloomed in 2009. The name refers to the
planting field where the seedling germinated and
grew. Introduced by Pépinières de Kervilou
(Béréhouc), of Quimper. Growth rate is medium,
resulting in an upright, bushy plant. Flower buds
are green and oval-shaped. The plant shows
moderate abundance of blooms in the course of the
mid-season flowering period. The semi-double
blooms are medium size, and deep cerise pink, with
yellow stamens and filaments. Occasionally two
petals mix with the stamens or pink marbled white
petaloids in a circle. Spent flower falls whole. Light
green and oval leaves average L9cm and W6cm.

- C. 'Lineostic Braz'
(*C. japonica*) Reg. No. 160. *C. japonica* seedling of
unknown parentage. Originated in 1993 by
Joséphine Béréhouc, of Quimper, Brittany, France;
first bloomed in 1998. The name refers to the
planting field in which the seedling germinated and
grew; this is the largest flower from the field.
Introduced by Pépinières de Kervilou (Béréhouc),
of Quimper. Growth rate is moderate for this bushy,
dense plant. Flower buds are oval and green. The
long flowering season extends from the beginning
of March to end of May with a floriferous display of
blooms. The rose-form double bloom is large (up to
W12cm), and light orchid pink, showing some
yellow stamens. The flowers exhibit a remarkable
contrast of dark shiny leaves with the bright pink
colour of the blooms. Spent flowers fall whole.

Large leaves are oval to elliptic, and average L11cm and W5.5cm; they are dark green, tough and thick, with shallow teeth around the margins.

• C. 'Perle de l'Odet'

(*C. japonica*) Reg. No. 161. *C. japonica* of unknown parentage. Seedling of 1993 originated by Joséphine Béréhouc, of Quimper, Brittany, France; first bloomed in 1998. The Odet River flows through the town of Quimper. Introduced by Pépinières de Kervilou (Béréhouc), of Quimper. On 17 March 2017, it was "baptized" in honour of the centennial of the Breton camellia association, the Société d'Horticulture Quimper. The plant exhibits an average growth rate, and an upright and bushy habit. Flower buds are light green and oval. Flowering is floriferous, through mid-season. The blooms are semi-double and cup-shaped, with yellow stamens mixed in a packet with the petals; filaments are white. The medium-sized flowers are soft pink with bright red streaks and scratches; the mottling background colour may vary to darker pink or red. Spent flowers fall whole. Leaves are medium sized, green and oval.

• C. 'Peter Totty'

(*C. × williamsii*) Reg. No. 162. Sport of C. × willliamsii 'Jill Totty', first observed in 1998, and first propagated by cuttings in 1999 by Mrs Jill Totty, Hampshire, UK. It has been exhibited at camellia shows in the UK. The plant shows medium growth rate, with upright, open arching growth habit. Flower buds are pale green, elliptic, tapering to a point at both ends. A long flowering begins in mid-season, and the plant is reliably floriferous. Semi-double to loose peony form blooms are rose-pink, with loose arrangement of stamens. Stamens are white with yellow anthers, filaments white, and petaloids pink and pink-streaked white. Flowers medium to large, up to 12cm. Spent flowers fall whole. Camellia fruit appear in moderate quantities, approximately 2cm, round and mid-green. Leaves are dark green, flat and medium size (average L10cm and W4cm).

• Philip

(*C. japonica*) Reg. No. 163. *C. japonica* of unknown parentage. Seedling of 1973 originated by WGT Hyde, at Woodlands Nursery Gardens, Dorset, UK; first bloomed 1983. Named by Mrs Rosemary

Legrand, of Dorset, UK, for Philip Legrand, grandson of WGT Hyde. Introduced at "new hybrids" class at the Spring Competition of the Royal Horticultural Society Garden, Wisley, UK, in 2014 and won First Prize. Growth habit is average, and bushy. Flower buds are oval, Colour 46A in the RHS 1966 Colour Chart Red Group. The plant, of consistent and floriferous blooming flowers in mid-season spring. Blooms are single and flat, large (average 10cm) with a central Higo-like boss of very long stamens; stamens are yellow-orange, and filaments yellow. The petals are bright red, Colour 53C in the RHS chart Red Group. Blooms fall whole when spent. The leaf is Colour 146A in the Yellow-Green Group of the RHS colour chart; elliptic, of medium size; margins recurved.

• **Sourire d'Annie** ('Annie's Smile')
(*C. japonica*) Reg. No. 164. Open-pollinated seedling of *C. japonica* 'Sylva' first appeared in 2011, and first bloomed in 2019. Originated and registered by Jean François Saint Jalm, of Seglien, France. Growth is upright and dense, with medium but vigorous growth rate. Flower buds are round and red 53B in the RHS colour chart of 2007. Blooming runs from February to May, with a very floriferous display. Blooms are anemone-form, and bright deep red-pink, colour 53B in the RHS chart Red Group; the petaloids are the same colour. The many stamens are yellow, with pink filaments. Flowers are medium-to-large, 8-9 cm in width; spent blooms remain on the plant. The flat leaves are medium green, with apiculate tips and medium serration, ranging from L7–10cm and W3–5.6 cm.

• **Spring Ruby**
(*C. japonica*) Reg. No. 165. Open pollinated *C. japonica* 'Bob Hope', seedling appeared in 2010, first bloomed in 2015. Originated by Joséphine Béréhouc, of Quimper, Brittany, France. Introduced by Pépinières de Kervilou (Béréhouc), of Quimper. Plant growth is at an average rate; upright and bushy. Oval flower buds. The cultivar has a late blooming season, with a moderate floral display. Formal double blooms are medium-size (W9cm), and deep purple-red. Outer petals are round, and inner petals narrow and elliptical. Spent blooms shatter. Leaves are medium size (L8cm, W4cm), dark green, oval, thick, with visible venations.

• **1001 Summer Nights Jasmine**
(*C. azalea* × *C. reticulata*) Reg. No. 166. Cross between unnamed seedling of *C. azalea* × *C. reticulata* 'Dr. Clifford Parks', seedling of 2001. Originated by Palm Eco-town Development Co, (Guangzhou, China). Breeder's reference 'Yulan01'. Introduced in Thompson & Morgan (UK) 2020 autumn catalogue. Plant is compact, bushy and dense, of rapid growth habit. Glossy green foliage. Semi-double, large, flowers vary from light pink to bright red. Blooms early summer to late autumn. Good garden performance, tolerates full sunlight.

Rhododendron, Camellia & Magnolia Group Trustees, Committees & Branch Chairmen 2021–2022

Index

Exbury
GARDENS
& Steam Railway

Now celebrating more than 100 years, Exbury Gardens is a spectacular collection of landscaped woodland, herbaceous, contemporary and formal gardens. At over 200 acres, these impressive gardens border the Beaulieu River and boasts a narrow-gauge steam railway, a refurbished restaurant and an outdoor cafe.

World-famous for the Rothschild collection of camellias, azaleas and magnolias. Exbury is also the birthplace of many rhododendron hybrids, all of which bloom in a decadent display of colour during April and May.

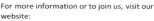